The Limits of Thought

The Limits of Thought
Discussions

J. Krishnamurti and David Bohm

London and New York

First published 1999
by Routledge
11 New Fetter Lane, London EC4P 4EE

Simultaneously published in the USA and Canada
by Routledge
29 West 35th Street, New York, NY 10001

Edited by R. McCoy

Typeset in Times by Routledge
Printed and bound in Great Britain by
Clays Ltd, St Ives PLC

British Library Cataloguing in Publication Data
A catalogue record for this book is available from the British Library

Library of Congress Cataloging-in-Publication Data
Krishnamurti, J. (Jiddu), 1895–
The limits of thought/discussions
p. cm.
1. Krishnamurti, J. (Jiddu), 1895–1986–Interviews. 2. Philosophy.
I. Bohm, David. II. Title.
B5134.K754A5 1999
181'.4–dc21   98–35092
                                                                    CIP

ISBN 0–415–19397–4 (hbk)
ISBN 0–415–19398–2 (pbk)

Contents

Foreword

The friendly relationship between David Bohm and J. Krishnamurti spanned almost a quarter of a century, during which they frequently had dialogues about the sources of individual and collective conflict, and the possibilities of freedom from self-centred and confusing activity through a certain quality of insight. Their discussions sometimes included other teachers and scientists, psychiatrists and scholars.

For some years David Bohm was a Trustee of the Krishnamurti Foundation and of Brockwood Park, the international school in Hampshire founded by Krishnamurti. From Brockwood's beginnings in 1969 almost until he died in 1992, David Bohm, at Krishnamurti's request, was vitally involved in the work of the school.

Some of the deep and sustained dialogues between Krishnamurti and David Bohm have been made available in publications and recordings. Those which comprise this collection, *The Limits of Thought*, shed further light on their challenging explorations of the nature of consciousness and the condition of humanity.

Mary Cadogan and Ray McCoy

Preface

An introduction to Krishnamurti's work

My first acquaintance with Krishnamurti's work was in 1959 when I read his book *The First and Last Freedom*. What particularly aroused my interest was his deep insight into the question of the observer and the observed. This question had long been close to the centre of my own work as a theoretical physicist who was primarily interested in the meaning of the quantum theory. In this theory, for the first time in the development of physics, the notion that the observer and the observed cannot be separated has been put forth as necessary for the understanding of the fundamental laws of matter in general. Because of this, as well as because the book contained many other deep insights, I felt that it was urgent for me to talk with Krishnamurti directly and personally as soon as possible. And when I first met him on one of his visits to London, I was struck by the great ease of communication with him, which was made possible by the intense energy with which he listened and by the freedom from self-protective reservations and barriers with which he responded to what I had to say. As a person who works in science I felt completely at home with this sort of response, because it was in essence of the same quality as that which I had met in contacts with other scientists with whom there had been a very close meeting of minds. And here I think especially of Einstein, who showed a similar intensity and absence of barrier in a number of discussions that took place between him and me. After this, I began to meet Krishnamurti regularly and to discuss with him whenever he came to London.

We began an association which since then has become closer, as I became interested in the schools which were set up through his initiative. In these discussions, we went quite deeply into many questions which concerned me in my scientific work. We probed into the nature of space and time, and of the universal, both with regard to external nature and with regard to mind. But then we went on to consider the general disorder and confusion that pervades the consciousness of mankind. It is here that I encountered what I feel to be Krishnamurti's major discovery. What he was seriously proposing is that all this disorder, which is the root cause of such widespread sorrow and misery, and which prevents human beings from properly working together, has its root in the fact that we are ignorant of the general nature of our own processes of thought. Or, to put it differently, it may be said that we do not see what is actually happening when we are engaged in the activity of thinking. Through close attention to and observation of this activity of thought, Krishnamurti feels that he directly perceives that thought is a material process which is going on inside of the human being in the brain and nervous system as a whole.

Ordinarily, we tend to be aware mainly of the content of this thought rather than of how it actually takes place. One can illustrate this point by considering what happens when one is reading a book. Usually, one is attentive almost entirely to the meaning of what is being read. However, one can also be aware of the book itself, of its constitution as being made up out of pages that can be turned, of the printed words and of the ink, of the fabric of the paper, etc. Similarly, we may be aware of the actual structure and function of the process of thought, and not merely of its content.

How can such an awareness come about? Krishnamurti proposes that this requires what he calls meditation. Now the word meditation has been given a wide range of different and even contradictory meanings, many of them involving rather superficial kinds of mysticism. Krishnamurti has in mind a definite and clear notion when he uses this word. One can obtain a valuable indication of this meaning by considering the derivation of the word. (The roots of words, in conjunction with their present generally accepted meanings, often yield surprising insight into their deeper meanings.) The English word meditation is based on the Latin root 'med', 'to measure'. The present meaning of this word is 'to reflect', 'to ponder' (i.e. to weigh or measure), and 'to give close attention'. Similarly, the Sanskrit word for meditation, which is 'dhyana', is closely related to 'dhyati', meaning 'to reflect'. So, at this rate, to meditate would be 'to ponder, to reflect, while giving close attention to what is actually going on as one does so'.

This is perhaps what Krishnamurti means by the beginning of meditation. That is to say, one gives close attention to all that is happening in conjunction with the actual activity of thought, which is the underlying source of the general disorder. One does this without choice, without criticism, without acceptance or rejection of what is going on. And all of this takes place along with reflections on the meaning of what one is learning about the activity of thought. (It is perhaps rather like reading a book in which the pages have been scrambled up, and being intensely aware of this disorder, rather than just 'trying to make sense' of the confused content that arises when one just accepts the pages as they happen to come.)

Krishnamurti has observed that the very act of meditation will, in itself, bring order to the activity of thought without the intervention of will, choice, decision, or any other action of the 'thinker'. As such order comes, the noise and chaos which are the usual background of our consciousness die out, and the mind becomes generally silent. (Thought arises only when needed for some genuinely valid purpose, and then stops, until needed again.)

In this silence, Krishnamurti says that something new and creative happens, something that cannot be conveyed in words, that is of extraordinary significance for the whole of life. So he does not attempt to communicate this verbally, but rather, he asks of those who are interested that they explore the question of meditation directly for themselves, through actual attention to the nature of thought.

Without attempting to probe into this deeper meaning of meditation, however, one can say that meditation, in Krishnamurti's sense of the word, can bring order to our overall mental activity, and this may be a key factor in bringing about an end to the sorrow, the misery, the chaos and confusion that have over the ages been the lot of mankind, and that are still generally continuing, without visible prospect of fundamental change for the foreseeable future.

Krishnamurti's work is permeated by what may be called the essence of the scientific approach, when this is considered in its very highest and purest form. Thus, he begins from a fact: this fact about the nature of our thought processes. This fact is established through close attention, involving careful listening to the process of consciousness, and observing it assiduously. In this, one is constantly learning, and out of this learning comes insight into the overall or general nature of the process of thought. This insight is then tested. First, one sees whether it holds together in a rational order. And then one sees whether it leads to order and coherence, on what flows out of it in life as a whole.

Krishnamurti constantly emphasizes that he is in no sense an authority. He has made certain discoveries, and he is simply doing his best to make these discoveries accessible to all those who are able to listen. His work does not contain a body of doctrine, nor does he offer techniques or methods for obtaining a silent mind. He is not aiming to set up any new system of religious belief. Rather, it is up to each human being to see if he can discover for himself that to which Krishnamurti is calling attention, and to go on from here to make new discoveries on his own.

It is clear then that an introduction such as this can at best show how Krishnamurti's work has been seen by a particular person, a scientist, such as myself. To see in full what Krishnamurti means, it is necessary, of course, to go on and to read what he actually says, with that quality of attention to the totality of one's responses, inward and outward, which we have been discussing here.

David Bohm

Part I

Against the pressures of tradition

1 Living in truth

KRISHNAMURTI: Where shall we start, sir?

DAVID BOHM: Do you have any ideas?

KRISHNAMURTI: Lots of them. If truth is something totally different from reality, then what place has action in daily life in relation to truth and reality? Can we talk about that?

DAVID BOHM: Yes.

KRISHNAMURTI: One would like to or one should or one has to act in truth. The action of reality is entirely different from the action of truth. Now, what is the action of truth? Is that action unrelated to the past, unrelated to an idea, an ideal? And therefore out of time? Is there ever an action out of time, or are actions always involved in time?

DAVID BOHM: Can you say that the truth acts in reality? That is, although reality may have no effect on truth, truth has some effect on reality?

KRISHNAMURTI: Yes. But one would like to find out if one lives in truth, not in the truth of reality, but in that truth which is not related to reality. Reality is a process of thought, of thinking about something that is real or reflected upon, or distorted, such as illusion.

So what is action in truth? If it is not related to reality, if it is not an action in the movement of time, what is action then? Is there such action? Can my mind dissociate itself from the past and from the idea of 'I shall be', or 'I will be', or 'I must be' or 'I should be', which are projections of my own desires? Is there an action that is totally separate from all that?

DAVID BOHM: Perhaps we are going very fast. I think ordinarily the action is related to the fact.

KRISHNAMURTI: Yes, we said fact is that which is being made or that which is being done *now*.

DAVID BOHM: There is another meaning – that which is actually proceeding or that which is actually established by perception or by experience.

KRISHNAMURTI: Which is now.

DAVID BOHM: Yes.

KRISHNAMURTI: The seeing is the doing. Perceiving is the acting in the present. And is the present a continuous movement of the past through the present to the future, or is the present a thing that is whole, that is complete, that is sane, healthy, holy – everything conveyed by that word 'whole'?

I think this is rather important to find out, because if a man wants to live in truth, this is his first question: what is action in relation to truth? I know action in relation to reality, which is based on memory, on environment, on circumstances, on adaptation, or which is an action to do something in the future.

DAVID BOHM: Is there a separation between truth and action?

KRISHNAMURTI: That's it.

DAVID BOHM: Is there a relationship, or is it the truth which acts?

KRISHNAMURTI: Yes. That's right. Is truth action or does truth act unrelated to time?

DAVID BOHM: It acts unrelated to time, but it is action itself.

KRISHNAMURTI: That's as we have said, perceiving is the doing.

DAVID BOHM: Yes, truth is what establishes the fact.

KRISHNAMURTI: And the fact is not only what is being done, what is being made, but the actuality of the moment.

DAVID BOHM: Yes. It is the actual act of perception which establishes the fact.

KRISHNAMURTI: That's right. So is perception a movement of time, a thing that comes from the past to the present and the future? Or is perception unrelated to that?

DAVID BOHM: I'd say it is unrelated.

KRISHNAMURTI: Yes. So are we saying that perception is action, and action is truth, and that truth is the perception of the actual, the *what is*, the moment?

DAVID BOHM: There is a peculiar history of that, because the pragmatists have said either that the truth is that which works or that the truth works. The working is not the same as the truth.

KRISHNAMURTI: Yes. Quite.

DAVID BOHM: There is a moment of time between the truth and how it works, in that view.

KRISHNAMURTI: That's wrong. The moment you have a gap, you...

DAVID BOHM: Yes, so the truth is action itself.

KRISHNAMURTI: Can a human being let truth operate?

DAVID BOHM: Would you say that the action, the operation of truth in reality, is intelligence?

KRISHNAMURTI: Yes. It must be, of course.

DAVID BOHM: Because in some sense intelligence is an action of truth.

KRISHNAMURTI: It is not cultivable.

DAVID BOHM: It is very difficult. We have discussed intelligence before, and in some way we seem to be discussing truth in the role that we were previously giving intelligence. It is very hard to make these words clear.

KRISHNAMURTI: Yes. What is the root meaning of that word 'truth'?

DAVID BOHM: We discussed it last time we met. I looked it up carefully since then. The English word 'true' has the root meaning 'honest', 'faithful'. And the Latin word 'verus' means 'that which is'. I think both meanings are rather significant.

KRISHNAMURTI: Yes.

DAVID BOHM: I am saying that reality must be honest and faithful; that is, like the machine that runs true. The word 'true' in English does not have quite the same meaning as 'verus' in Latin, or it has other shades of meaning.

KRISHNAMURTI: Verus – that which is – of course. Sir, what I am trying to get at is whether a human being can live only in the present – in the sense that we are talking of the present. That is, to live with *what is* all the time, and not with what should be or what will be or what has been.

DAVID BOHM: I think the principal question is whether one can be clear on that which is not, but which appears to be that which is.

KRISHNAMURTI: Quite. Therefore we should go back, sir, to what perception is. If I can perceive reality clearly – all the illusions and the actual, the reasonableness and the unreasonableness of reality – if I see that clearly, then can there be a perception of *what is*, which we say is truth? That very perception is an action in which there is no operation of thought. Is that what we are trying to say?

DAVID BOHM: Yes. When we say perception of *what is*, then that is separation again.

KRISHNAMURTI: It is not; there is no observer and the observed, there is only perception.

DAVID BOHM: It is very hard in the language to avoid this, because, as I see it, the perception, or the fact, is *what is*. The act is what is.

KRISHNAMURTI: Yes. Are you saying, sir, that the *what is* has its own action?

DAVID BOHM: Yes, or it is its action.

KRISHNAMURTI: That is it. It is its own action. Yes.

DAVID BOHM: We have to be careful because the language continually tends to put in separation. We tend to think things are real and have some substance; that is, that they exist in themselves. We tend to think that *what is* is reality and that truth would only be correct knowledge about reality. But what we are proposing here is to turn it around to say that truth is *what is*, and reality as a whole is nothing but appearances. Reality is a kind of appearance that may be a correct appearance or that may be incorrect, may be an illusion. There is a tremendous habit to say that reality is *what is*.

KRISHNAMURTI: We have said that reality is a projection of thought, of what we think about, reflect upon. And anything that thought creates, makes, is a reality either as a distortion or as an actuality. We accept that. And we were trying to find out the relationship between truth and reality. Is there a connection between the two?

That's one point. And the other is: is there an action that is different from the action of reality, that is the action of truth – no, not action of truth but truth acting? Whereas there is a division in reality.

DR PARCHURE: A division of what?

KRISHNAMURTI: Between the observer and the observed.

DAVID BOHM: Yes, the observer is one reality observing the other reality. But truth is indivisible.

KRISHNAMURTI: So is there an action in one's life which is indivisible? If the mind cannot find that indivisible action, it must always be in time, in conflict, in sorrow, and in all that follows from that.

DAVID BOHM: One could think that reality is a field which contains all the things that might be there. It contains thought, and thought is real, and all these things react to each other and reflect on each other.

KRISHNAMURTI: They are interrelated.

DAVID BOHM: They interrelate by reaction and reflection. So my thought is not different from all the interrelations.

KRISHNAMURTI: If thought has created them, they are all interrelated.

DAVID BOHM: Now, if we look at nature, one view of nature says it's real, but something beyond that seems to be implied.

KRISHNAMURTI: No, that tree *is*, therefore it is truth; but I can distort it.

DAVID BOHM: That's the point I want to get at. If we say that the tree is that which is and is truth, we are in a way saying truth is a substance.

KRISHNAMURTI: I see.

DAVID BOHM: We are seeking a substance, something, that stands under the appearances. We seek it in reality. It has been the age-long habit to look for some solid, permanent reality that underlies all the changes and explains them so that we understand. But it may be that the whole of reality is no substance. Perhaps it does not have an independent existence, is a field, and what stands under this reality is truth. Would that make sense to you?

KRISHNAMURTI: But that would lead us to a great danger.

DAVID BOHM: There's a danger in that. Is there any way of making this point clear?

KRISHNAMURTI: The inner is the truth. Are you saying that?

DAVID BOHM: Not exactly, no. We are saying that truth is action.

KRISHNAMURTI: Yes, truth is action. Perception is action, seeing is action.

DAVID BOHM: If you say the tree is truth, the actuality of the tree is the action of the tree. But this turns it around. It is very hard. Because of our customary use of language, it gets confused quickly. One turns around the other way and tends to think that the tree is the reality and that I see it.

KRISHNAMURTI: Yes. The seeing is the action.

DAVID BOHM: Now, we have to get hold of this very subtle new thing by a new approach and right use of language. You say the seeing of the tree is the truth.

KRISHNAMURTI: Is the action.

DAVID BOHM: Would you say that the seeing is the tree?

KRISHNAMURTI: In seeing the tree is the action.

DAVID BOHM: Yes, seeing is the action. Does the tree have any action in itself?

KRISHNAMURTI: Obviously it's growing or it's dying or...

DAVID BOHM: That's the point I'm trying to get clear, because if you only talk about the seeing as the action, the question is always in the back of your mind: what about the rest of the action?

KRISHNAMURTI: I understand.

DAVID BOHM: We are trying to understand this and I see a problem. I say, seeing the tree is action; that is very clear. Then I begin to see that the tree has its own action, although I don't see it.

KRISHNAMURTI: Of course, which I don't see.

DAVID BOHM: And I ask what about that, how do I consider that?

KRISHNAMURTI: Why should I consider it?

DAVID BOHM: Well, to understand. For example, you think the tree is growing.

KRISHNAMURTI: Then that becomes the process of thought: how to feed it, how to help it to grow better, how to shelter it, and so on.

DAVID BOHM: Yes, but you see we tend to get into the situation of saying that only what we see at this moment has any significance. And I want to put it so that we do justice to the other thing without contradicting any of this. I don't know how.

KRISHNAMURTI: Now, let's begin again. We say seeing is action.

DAVID BOHM: Yes, there is no doubt about that.

KRISHNAMURTI: Seeing the tree is action. But the tree, the actuality, has its own activity.

DAVID BOHM: And other people have their own action or activity when I don't see them.

KRISHNAMURTI: That tree has its own activity. Now, thought can come along and help it to grow properly, feed it and so on. Why should there be a division between seeing, acting, and the tree growing?

DAVID BOHM: I don't think there should be.

KRISHNAMURTI: Sir, we said earlier, seeing, acting, is intelligence. Truth acting in the field of reality is intelligence.

DAVID BOHM: Yes.

KRISHNAMURTI: Wait a minute, I want to get this clear.

DAVID BOHM: Is that right?

KRISHNAMURTI: I'm not sure it's right. I want to question it. But truth *is* intelligence.

DAVID BOHM: That's another way of looking at it. One could propose that truth is intelligence.

KRISHNAMURTI: Yes, because the seeing is the acting; that action is whole, and therefore it is intelligence. Any action that is whole must be intelligence.

DAVID BOHM: To use two words suggests you are looking at it in two different ways. I'm not clear what the difference is.

KRISHNAMURTI: Would it be right if I said seeing is the doing and therefore it is intelligence and that intelligence is the essence of truth? That intelligence operates in all the field?

DAVID BOHM: Intelligence operates in all the field, but if you say intelligence is the essence of truth, it is not clear.

KRISHNAMURTI: Essence of truth in the sense of the seeing is the doing. The seeing *what is*, is action. That action operates through intelligence.

DAVID BOHM: Well, now we have made a kind of distinction. It's not very clear.

KRISHNAMURTI: I want to find out if it is possible to live entirely in truth. If we start from there, perhaps we can go into it. That is, one is functioning only with *what is*, one is not bringing into operation his memories, his personal reactions and all that, but lets the fact act.

Sir, would you say, if one were living in truth and therefore living with that capacity of intelligence, that intelligence operates in the field of reality?

DAVID BOHM: And also beyond it.

KRISHNAMURTI: Because it is beyond it, because it is outside reality.

DAVID BOHM: Yes, intelligence is the action of truth, but it cannot actually be in the field of reality.

KRISHNAMURTI: That is all that we are saying.

(Pause)

DAVID BOHM: We are saying that reality is a field which should be 'true' in the sense of being straight, healthy, sane and so on, not distorted. Now, we don't know what this field of reality is. I propose that in some sense it is not a substance, it doesn't stand by itself, but truth can operate in that field.

KRISHNAMURTI: Yes, intelligently.

DAVID BOHM: And so far there is no problem. But when we try to say, 'Does the tree have its own action when we are not looking at it?', then we begin to produce a problem.

KRISHNAMURTI: Of course, when we're not looking at it, it's going on.

DAVID BOHM: Yes, it's going on, but then we have to say that that's part of the field of reality; we accept the field of reality as operating.

KRISHNAMURTI: Yes.

Sir, you live in truth and your actions in reality are guided by intelligence. And I as an observer observe you, the observed – as two different entities – and I want to find out how to live in a sane way, which means to have no contradiction, to live always with *what is*. How am I to come to that? I see enormous possibilities in what you are. I don't know if I am making myself clear. I see that is a real, creative way of living. And whatever you do, whatever you say, whatever you write has got that quality. Not that I'm greedy or that I am envious of you, but I say: 'What a marvellous thing it is to have that capacity'.

Now how am I, who have always thought in duality, as the observer and the observed, to come to that? Because if it is something unique to you, then I've no interest.

DAVID BOHM: Yes, it can't be unique or it won't be true.

KRISHNAMURTI: That's just it. So how am I – not how as a method – how is one to get that thing? I want to live the way you do. I see that I can't imitate you, you're not my example, but there must be that same perfume in me as you have. You follow, sir? From your discussion I am beginning to understand the field of reality and truth, which is the seeing of *what is*. The seeing of what is, that intelligence, can operate in this area of reality. And because it is intelligent it will never distort that reality, it will never go off into a distorting activity. So I see that very clearly. I understand it verbally perhaps, intellectually, and I feel a little emotionally attracted to it. How am I to come to that?

DAVID BOHM: Truth is indivisible, which means that...

KRISHNAMURTI: Truth is indivisible, but I am divided, I am fragmented, I am broken up. I'm living in reality only.

DAVID BOHM: Well, I have to see the falseness of that. As truth arises one...

KRISHNAMURTI: Then you give me no hope; then I'm lost, I haven't got the ground to stand on. I know how to operate in reality, because I've been trained, conditioned, all that. Either I do it badly or excellently, rising above all that. But I haven't got this other thing.

DR PARCHURE: But another part of your reality is in the position of the state in which...

KRISHNAMURTI: No, I only know that reality. I've observed that reality being distorted. I've observed the energy of reality operating rationally and irrationally. I'm quite familiar with that.

DR PARCHURE: But then observing is doing.

KRISHNAMURTI: No, he tells me that but I don't know what that means. I understand it intellectually, I understand the verbal communication, but not the fact of it.

DAVID BOHM: When you say, for example, that you see that reality is distorted, it seems that therefore something is beyond reality.

KRISHNAMURTI: That's why I said I begin to see what distortion is.

DAVID BOHM: And to see that requires truth.

KRISHNAMURTI: Wait! Does it require truth? That's what I want to find out.

DAVID BOHM: Let's look into that. If there's no truth, then I don't see anything.

KRISHNAMURTI: That's what I want to get at. Is that the beginning, or the quality, of truth? Seeing the distorting factors in the field of reality?

DAVID BOHM: Seeing the false.

KRISHNAMURTI: The false, the neurotic, all the rest of it – is seeing that the seed of the other?

DAVID BOHM: It has to be. Because, if I see it and it's only reality seeing reality, then it has no meaning.

KRISHNAMURTI: Quite.

DR PARCHURE: That's not in the field of intelligence.

KRISHNAMURTI: No, sir, don't jump to anything. Having operated in the field of reality all one's life and seen the distortions in that field, the seeing of that distortion is truth. That's what I want to find out. Seeing the fact.

DAVID BOHM: That has to be truth.

DR PARCHURE: But you said the man living in reality only verbally understands this.

KRISHNAMURTI: No. I live in reality, reality being all the things thought has put together, all the activity of thought thinking about or reflecting upon something, distorted or rational. I've lived in all that, and here comes along, say, a doctor, who says, 'Look, truth is that which is'. And he says, 'When you see the distortion, that *is* the truth, that *is* action'.

DR PARCHURE: Such a person will not act.

KRISHNAMURTI: No, just listen, don't discuss with me yet. He says, in the field of reality, seeing distortion – which is the fact, that fact which is – that is truth. So you have told me that when you see without the observer, when you see that the observer and the observed is one, that *is* truth.

DAVID BOHM: We made a jump between seeing the distortion and seeing the observer and the observed as one. Ordinarily I would say I have seen that reality is distorted, but at that moment I still don't see that the observer and the observed is one; there seems to be a jump.

KRISHNAMURTI: Right, I jumped, yes. Sir, how do I see distortion? Is the seeing of distortion a reasoned process? Or is it...?

DAVID BOHM: It's instantaneous, it's without time.

KRISHNAMURTI: Yes, without time.

DAVID BOHM: Perhaps we should go slowly on that, because sometimes one feels that it comes in a flash, but sometimes the seeing comes so gradually that you don't know when it comes. It seems both of those are different ways of experiencing *what is*, out of time.

KRISHNAMURTI: Can it come gradually?

DAVID BOHM: It seems to, I'm not saying it does. But when you think it over you never know exactly how it comes. Sometimes it seems that it came in a flash, but sometimes it came in so gradually you don't know exactly when you understood it. But being out of time means we don't say 'in a flash' or...

KRISHNAMURTI: Just a minute, sir, I want to see. The seeing is the doing. Therefore there is no gradual way.

DAVID BOHM: No, there's no gradual way, but I think if you say, 'in a flash', you also bring in time.

KRISHNAMURTI: Of course.

DAVID BOHM: If you say it's sudden, you bring in time. If you say it's gradual, you bring in time. So you can't say either.

KRISHNAMURTI: But would you put it this way? The seeing is the doing; it has already been done. And you want to find reasons for it.

DAVID BOHM: You want to explain it in terms of reality.

KRISHNAMURTI: That's it.

DAVID BOHM: You see, you're slipping back into the notion that reality is what is, and truth is merely explaining, giving information about reality. In the usual situation somebody sees distortion, but he may find out that he's still not free of it and therefore time has come in.

KRISHNAMURTI: Then he's not seeing. If I'm not free of my distortion, though I see it, I haven't seen it.

DAVID BOHM: Yes. He hasn't seen the whole of it.

KRISHNAMURTI: And seeing is the whole.

DAVID BOHM: It is the whole, but I think this point needs to be worked on very carefully, because what generally happens is one sees, but not the whole, and then one asks you, 'What am I to do in that situation?' I saw the distortion, but it still seems to come back. How shall I see the whole of it?

KRISHNAMURTI: You can't see the whole of it.

DAVID BOHM: Then how shall I see it so that it won't come back?

KRISHNAMURTI: Sir, I think the catch is in this: is seeing/doing a thought process?

DAVID BOHM: No, of course not.

KRISHNAMURTI: You say it is not; the thought process only comes in during the explanation. The seeing is the doing, which means seeing the whole. It must be, otherwise it's not seeing. And if the mind sees the whole, then the distortion can never come back.

DAVID BOHM: Yes, I have to see the whole field of reality, because that's where the distortion is. Let's say I see the distortion occurring in certain activities, in certain cases I see that I distort. But that is not yet seeing the whole field of reality, so I have to see the *whole* field of reality.

KRISHNAMURTI: I think you do, sir. When you see and the seeing is the doing, you must see the whole.

DAVID BOHM: Yes, what I mean is, see the essence of this field, not every little detail.

KRISHNAMURTI: No, of course not. Can one say what that act of intelligence is in the field of reality?

DAVID BOHM: I don't quite understand the question.

KRISHNAMURTI: Can one predict that state? Can one tell another verbally what that intelligence will do in the field of reality? Can one communicate, or state beforehand, what it will do?

I see this truth operating in the field of reality is intelligence. Now, what will that intelligence do under certain circumstances? Can one ask that, or is it a distorted question?

DAVID BOHM: Well, it's somewhat distorted. It rather presupposes that the intelligence is one reality and what is operating is another.

KRISHNAMURTI: Yes. So that is what we are doing all the time: 'Tell me what that intelligence will do in the field of reality and I will follow that.' You have that intelligence, and I ask you, pray to you, to tell me how that intelligence, how the truth operates in the field of reality.

DAVID BOHM: I think you could say that intelligence may be operating in the actions of one man. I don't know if it would be fair to say that, rather than saying he has the intelligence.

KRISHNAMURTI: Sir, what place has love in truth?

DAVID BOHM: Well, it's difficult to know exactly what the question means.

KRISHNAMURTI: The question means, is what is generally called love always in the field of reality?

DAVID BOHM: I don't think it could be basically in the field of reality.

KRISHNAMURTI: But we have reduced it to that.

DAVID BOHM: It could operate in the field of reality.

KRISHNAMURTI: So what is love and truth? Is truth love? That word 'love', what does it mean, sir?

DAVID BOHM: From the dictionary the meaning is very unclear. But aside from pleasure and so on which is the basic root...

KRISHNAMURTI: That's all reality, of course.

DAVID BOHM: The nearest I could get to it was 'goodwill and benevolence to all'.

KRISHNAMURTI: Compassion.

DAVID BOHM: Compassion, goodwill, benevolence. But most of the meanings go back to various forms of pleasure.

KRISHNAMURTI: Quite right. Is pleasure in the field of reality?

DAVID BOHM: Yes.

KRISHNAMURTI: It is. Then that pleasure has no relation to truth.

DAVID BOHM: Well, you could say that in genuine enjoyment there's a kind of pleasure which...

KRISHNAMURTI: Is enjoyment pleasure?

DAVID BOHM: It depends on how you use the words. If you want to, you can establish a distinction of the word and say it is not. But there may be an apparent similarity between the two.

KRISHNAMURTI: There is enjoyment in seeing the tree. Not that 'I am enjoying the tree', but the seeing of that tree is a joy. Therefore the seeing is the doing, and the doing is joy.

DAVID BOHM: Yes, good so far.

KRISHNAMURTI: Then what place has compassion in the field of reality? If we said compassion is love, truth...

DAVID BOHM: Then that's all part of the action of truth, isn't it? It's all in the action of truth.

KRISHNAMURTI: Right. This becomes very difficult.

DAVID BOHM: The words are difficult. If you say love is in the action of truth, the action of truth includes, at the very least, benevolence and compassion.

KRISHNAMURTI: It's all one, isn't it? Seeing, doing, compassion – it's all one. Not 'seeing, then doing, then compassion'. Seeing and the doing is the whole. And then there is that seeing as the whole. In that there is compassion.

DAVID BOHM: The truth is whole and indivisible. The lack of compassion can only arise from the division. In other words, there is a sense of division.

KRISHNAMURTI: Yes. Lack of compassion.

DAVID BOHM: If man feels divided from other people or nature, then he will not have compassion. So if there is no division...

KRISHNAMURTI: That is compassion.

DAVID BOHM: ...compassion is inevitable.

KRISHNAMURTI: Yes, so it's all one.

DAVID BOHM: Yes. Which means, if you say there is a particular personal feature of reality, then it implies division.

KRISHNAMURTI: Again – seeing, doing, truth, love – all that is love. Let's call it that for the moment. Because I feel compassionate in that sense, I love you. You don't become a particular thing – I love you.

DAVID BOHM: That isn't quite clear, because there's the tremendous tendency to particularize.

KRISHNAMURTI: When I separate you, in that separation love cannot exist.

DAVID BOHM: What do you mean by 'me' without separation?

KRISHNAMURTI: When the thought process operates in me, as 'me' and 'not me', when there is that sense of duality, is there love, is there compassion?

DAVID BOHM: No, because in that there is separation.

KRISHNAMURTI: Then when there is the perception of the whole – which is love – I love you. And I have the same feeling also for the other.

DAVID BOHM: What meaning do we give to people or things when we perceive the whole?

KRISHNAMURTI: I've known you and the others for years. When I love you it doesn't mean I exclude the others. I'll live with you, I'll cook for you, you are my wife, or whatever it is, but the others are not excluded.

DAVID BOHM: I understand that, but it seems there is some truth too in distinguishing certain people even if we don't exclude the others.

KRISHNAMURTI: Of course, there must be.

DAVID BOHM: There may be a distinction with no exclusion. I'm trying to get at something, because...

KRISHNAMURTI: Go ahead, sir, keep talking, because this is one of the problems. When we say 'I love you', we have made that love into an exclusive process. You are mine, I am yours, with all the dependency, and all that follows. When I see dependency, then I see the structure of dependency as a whole; and therefore the seeing is the doing, it is finished.

DAVID BOHM: Are you and I a reality?

KRISHNAMURTI: Of course.

DAVID BOHM: Is that what you mean? To a certain extent you and I are realities, and I have love for you and for another, and for some thing in reality. In other words, it seems there is a relation, that love is an action of truth in reality.

KRISHNAMURTI: That's what we said. That is, when I see that I depend on you – which I call love – and I see the whole nature of dependency, all the intricacies, then it's finished. Therefore I no longer depend – which doesn't mean callousness. And the seeing of that is compassion. Therefore I love you though I don't depend on you.

DAVID BOHM: Yes. To see that is necessary for compassion. We say it *is* compassion.

KRISHNAMURTI: But as long as I depend on you, the other thing is not.

DAVID BOHM: When I depend on you there is something false.

KRISHNAMURTI: Of course.

So what are we saying, sir? For a man who lives in reality and observes the rational and the irrational in that field, the seeing of the irrational is the truth because he sees the whole of the irrationality of that field.

DAVID BOHM: Yes, it's the essence.

KRISHNAMURTI: And because he sees it – the seeing is the doing – that is the truth. So he lives in truth in the field of reality.

DAVID BOHM: Yes. I think the basic thing that's false is when one person depends on another. In seeing the field of reality as something more than it actually is, he is giving it overwhelming importance.

KRISHNAMURTI: Quite.

DAVID BOHM: And therefore everything is distorted.

(Pause)

KRISHNAMURTI: So in a school, where a man is trying to convey something, how does he communicate it to the student? How does he communicate it to the world? How do you communicate this thing to a businessman? How do you communicate it to a priest who is living in reality and has created the image of God or Jesus, or whatever it is, which is a distortion? He *won't* see that.

DAVID BOHM: Well, isn't it possible to communicate the fact of distortion?

KRISHNAMURTI: Yes, you can, but it is…

DAVID BOHM: It meets resistance.

KRISHNAMURTI: There is such tremendous conditioning. That's what happens with most of the students, with anybody. How do you break down that resistance? Through compassion?

DAVID BOHM: I think it's necessary. It's necessary to have compassion.

KRISHNAMURTI: Wait. You are compassionate, and I am terribly conditioned. I believe deeply in various things. You may be very kind, gentle...

DAVID BOHM: I don't mean only that. I mean that I don't depend on you and I understand some of the things you talk about.

KRISHNAMURTI: Yes. How do you make me break this thing?

DAVID BOHM: I think what's needed is not just compassion, but an energy.

KRISHNAMURTI: That's what I'm coming to.

DAVID BOHM: Passion itself.

KRISHNAMURTI: Which means that one has that tremendous energy which is born of passion, compassion and all the rest of it. Does that energy bring about a new consciousness in the other? Or are we adding a new content to consciousness?

DAVID BOHM: No, I shouldn't think so. If you add a little content, wouldn't it be the same story?

KRISHNAMURTI: It would be the same thing, that's what I mean. I've listened to the Buddha, I've listened to Christ, to Judaism; I've listened to various things, and all these are the contents of my consciousness. And you come along and add some more to it. Because you are energetic, you are full of this thing, burning, and I absorb that, and add another candle to it – and you say, 'Don't do that'. But I've already done it because that's my habit, my conditioning – to add, to carry burden after burden. How do I receive you? How do I listen to you? What are you to do with me, sir?

   After all, you have this problem in your university. How are you to convey this sense of truth to a student? And you are burning with it, you are full of it. It must be a problem to you, you're beating your head against a wall. Fortunately, I'm not in that position because I don't care. I mean, I won't say, 'Do listen'; if they won't listen, they won't.

DAVID BOHM: That's more or less what I do.

KRISHNAMURTI: Do you bring a new quality into their consciousness? Look at Stalin, Lenin, Hitler, the priests in the name of Jesus, the Hindus, and so on, they have affected consciousness.

DAVID BOHM: Not in this fundamental way.

KRISHNAMURTI: No, but they have affected it, because they are priests, they have talked, they have influenced, they have mentally and physically tortured people. Are you influencing them here or are you adding another chapter to that consciousness?

DAVID BOHM: That is the danger.

KRISHNAMURTI: Or are you saying, 'Get out of all that'?

(Pause)

You see, that's just it. There is no seeing without freedom. Freedom is the essence of seeing – freedom from prejudice and so on. A mind that is free does see. The seeing is the doing.

DAVID BOHM: Yes, because the lack of freedom is the lack of seeing.

KRISHNAMURTI: Of course.

DAVID BOHM: We always move in a circle. The lack of freedom is the reality, is the instrument of reality.

KRISHNAMURTI: A Communist would say there is no such thing as freedom.

DAVID BOHM: I think that many Communists would not agree. Marx and Engels speak of ultimate freedom but they thought they could achieve freedom through reality, that by changing reality they would eventually arrive at freedom.

KRISHNAMURTI: Of course, Marx said, 'Change the environment', and so on.

DAVID BOHM: Yes, change the reality of man and he will be free. Of course the man who is not free cannot change his reality.

KRISHNAMURTI: Of course. So you see, that's the danger.

DAVID BOHM: But we have to step out of the whole thing.

KRISHNAMURTI: That's right, step out of the whole thing – and that needs energy. As long as I live in the field of reality, which has its own energy, that energy will not free me. But the seeing of the distortion in that field of reality will give energy.

DAVID BOHM: I think I prefer to say the seeing of the inevitability of distortion. Because one might see the distortion, and hope to avoid it.

KRISHNAMURTI: The seeing of the distortion is energy.

DAVID BOHM: Yes, and the distortion cannot be avoided in that field. There can be no way out of distortion in the field of reality.

KRISHNAMURTI: Are you saying that, in the field of reality, distortion is inevitable?

DAVID BOHM: Yes, as long as we stay in that field.

KRISHNAMURTI: Of course.

DAVID BOHM: I think that many people would say they agree that we distort, but at the back of our minds there is the hope that we can do something about it.

KRISHNAMURTI: Quite. The desire to stop it is another form of distortion.

DAVID BOHM: So I have to see that there is no way out in that field.

KRISHNAMURTI: Wait. In that field of reality there are distortions. The seeing of the distortions – seeing in the sense of seeing the whole of distortion – brings energy. Which means I cannot say there is no freedom from that distortion.

DAVID BOHM: The seeing of the distortion is energy. Couldn't we say that the feeling that there is no energy is also a distortion?

KRISHNAMURTI: Of course. We said that in that field of reality, reality has its own energy.

DAVID BOHM: It has a kind of energy, and I think that energy includes desire.

KRISHNAMURTI: Includes desire, includes all...

DAVID BOHM: All the forms of energy.

KRISHNAMURTI: And also the energy of distortion. Now to see that distortion, the mind must be free. It must put it outside, as it were, and look at it.

DAVID BOHM: Could I look at it like this? The whole field of reality is permeated with distortion. Now you are proposing that we can look in some way at this whole field of reality. You are saying that we can in some sense put it at a distance, make a separation. Is that what you are saying?

KRISHNAMURTI: Yes.

DAVID BOHM: We have to be very clear, because we are also saying there's no division.

KRISHNAMURTI: The observer and the observed, and all that.

DAVID BOHM: There seems to be a contradiction here and we have to try to clear it up. Is there a kind of space, or something in between? 'Between' might be the wrong word, but this reality...

KRISHNAMURTI: This reality is empty. This reality is nothing.

DAVID BOHM: Yes. We said it was 'no thing'. The word 'nothing' means no thing. So nothingness is 'no thingness', which is not reality. Reality is to be something.

KRISHNAMURTI: Quite.

DAVID BOHM: So if we say nothingness, it doesn't mean unreal – neither real nor unreal – but it is entirely out of that field.

KRISHNAMURTI: Quite.

DAVID BOHM: Ultimately reality is nothing, no thing. But now we're saying that there has to be a kind of space, of emptiness, of nothingness, in which the thing can be seen. Because seeing is truth, which is no thing, nothingness.

KRISHNAMURTI: That's right.

DAVID BOHM: And seeing can only take place in nothingness, which is energy.

KRISHNAMURTI: Yes. When the mind is empty, when the mind is nothing, not a thing, in that there is perception.

DAVID BOHM: Yes, and energy. The mind is nothing and reality is no thing ultimately. There is nothingness and in nothingness there is a sort of form which is reality – but a form which is nothing.

KRISHNAMURTI: Quite. But, sir, that presupposes that there is nothing.

DAVID BOHM: That's only an image.

KRISHNAMURTI: Of course, that's what I want to make clear.

DAVID BOHM: I mean it's an image too. Because if you held on to it you would turn nothing into a thing.

KRISHNAMURTI: And then begins the whole thing. Quite.

DAVID BOHM: But, as you say, in some way the mind steps back in order to see. It is not closely connected with reality. Would you say there's a space?

KRISHNAMURTI: There must be a space.

DAVID BOHM: I feel reality is in the space. Now when you say 'space', it means that there's room.

KRISHNAMURTI: Distance.

DAVID BOHM: The thing is not closely connected.

KRISHNAMURTI: Isn't there a space when the observer is the observed?

DAVID BOHM: We have to get it clear. It sounds wrong to say there is a space, it sounds like a separation.

KRISHNAMURTI: We are not using the word 'space' as a division, as a dividing factor.

DAVID BOHM: Can we make it clear?

KRISHNAMURTI: Of course. When I see something, a candle, there is the verbal space of distance, time, and all the rest of it; but the *seeing* has no space. I said, when people say 'I see', there is a division.

DAVID BOHM: But you said that we should be able to have some space between reality...

KRISHNAMURTI: We said there should be some space, not in the sense of a division.

DAVID BOHM: Yes, then we have to say there are two kinds of space, one is dividing and the other is not. This non-dividing space includes everything, would that be right?

KRISHNAMURTI: Yes. To see, and the doing – in that there is no division. Where there is division, there is so-called space of time and distance and all the rest of it. But in this there is no division and therefore it is in space.

DAVID BOHM: Yes, well, everything is in space.

KRISHNAMURTI: Of course.

DAVID BOHM: Space includes everything.

KRISHNAMURTI: Yes, of course, I exist.

DAVID BOHM: That space is not a division, you could almost call it the ground or the underlying substance.

KRISHNAMURTI: The space I create when I dislike you, or like you, is different from the freedom of space of this space.

DAVID BOHM: There is 'room', I would say. The room is one whole space, it goes into the outer space, and every object is in a sense in that space, united, all one.

KRISHNAMURTI: Yes, without space we couldn't exist. I wonder if we're talking of the same thing?

DAVID BOHM: Are we discussing the space of the mind as well?

KRISHNAMURTI: Yes, the space in the mind as well.

DAVID BOHM: As there is visual space, space which we can sense as one, there is the space in the mind. Can we say that reality is in the space in the mind?

KRISHNAMURTI: Reality is the space...

DAVID BOHM: Within.

KRISHNAMURTI: I can artificially create it.

DAVID BOHM: Yes, but when we say we see the whole of reality from a space, is this whole of reality within the space of the mind?

KRISHNAMURTI: Let's get this clear.

Look, seeing is acting. In that there is no space as division. I think that's clear. Therefore that space is the freedom of nothingness. We said that.

DAVID BOHM: Nothingness is the same as freedom, because so long as a thing is a thing, it is not free.

KRISHNAMURTI: Yes. Therefore truth is nothingness – not a thing. The action of nothingness, which is intelligence in the field of reality – that intelligence being free and all the rest of it – operates in reality without distortion. If in one's mind there is no space but it is crowded with problems, with images, with remembrances, with knowledge, such a mind is not free and therefore cannot see, and not seeing, cannot act. Because my mind is crowded, it is not free, there is no space.

DAVID BOHM: Yes, when there is no space, then the mind is controlled by all these things.

KRISHNAMURTI: Yes, controlled by environment, by distortions.

DAVID BOHM: And that continues to make distortions.

KRISHNAMURTI: So a mind that is empty, nothing, is capable of the seeing which is the doing; and the doing is truth and so on. Is that space limited because of the mind? Of course it's not limited, it can't be. It is not created by thought, therefore it's not limited.

DAVID BOHM: Yes, but this space can see the things of reality and act in relation to those things.

KRISHNAMURTI: Yes.

DAVID BOHM: So in some sense the thing can be absorbed or assimilated into that space. I mean that the space can relate to the thing.

KRISHNAMURTI: I don't quite follow, sir. Are you asking if reality exists in space?

DAVID BOHM: That's what I'm saying. Perhaps there is no reality in space, but in some sense there is the essence...

KRISHNAMURTI: That's right, sir, there's no reality in space.

DAVID BOHM: Yes, but there is some essence when you contact the thing; the thing is thought, we said, what we think about.

KRISHNAMURTI: That's right.

DAVID BOHM: This thought is understood in some way. I don't know exactly how to put it.

KRISHNAMURTI: Are we asking, sir, when there is space in the mind, what place has reality?

DAVID BOHM: Yes.

KRISHNAMURTI: Reality is the thing which is thought about. What place has thought in that truth, in that emptiness, in that space? What place has reality in that space? Has it any place? Has thought any place in that spacelessness?

DAVID BOHM: In some way the space seems to contact the field of thought. It takes action in that field.

KRISHNAMURTI: I understand. To make it much simpler for myself, what place has thought in that space?

DAVID BOHM: It may have no place.

KRISHNAMURTI: What is the relationship?

DAVID BOHM: Between that space and thought?

KRISHNAMURTI: Let's put it that way. What is the relationship between that space and thought. If thought had created that space, then it would have a relationship. But thought has not created that space.

DAVID BOHM: We are saying that truth can act in reality, but reality cannot act in truth. Therefore this space can act in reality or in thought, although it doesn't go the other way.

KRISHNAMURTI: Yes, it's a one-way ticket.

DAVID BOHM: And it acts primarily, as I said, to straighten it out. If it's straight, then thought can move on its own.

KRISHNAMURTI: That's right. So what is the relationship of that space to thought?

DAVID BOHM: To the content of thought, there is none. But in some sense thought is also within that which is. In other words, we said thought is a reality. When we say thought is not working right...

KRISHNAMURTI: Are you saying, sir, when the operation of thought is straight, rational, sane, healthy, holy, that has a relationship to this space?

DAVID BOHM: Yes, I'm implying that. In some way they are then parallel. But this space can also act within thought to help make it parallel.

KRISHNAMURTI: Yes, we said that. It's a one-way relationship.

DAVID BOHM: Yes, I am trying to make a distinction. If we take the content of thought, which is consciousness, then that has no action on the space. But I am trying to say that the distortion of thought goes beyond content.

KRISHNAMURTI: Why do you say 'beyond content'?

DAVID BOHM: I mean that it involves the way of working of thought. What is the action of truth within thought? That's really the question. In general you can see it's to straighten out the way of working, to remove all the distortions.

KRISHNAMURTI: Wait. Seeing is the doing, let's stick to that. The seeing of distortion is the ending of distortion. It's ended because of that energy of seeing.

DAVID BOHM: Yes, which acts somehow within thought or on thought.

KRISHNAMURTI: Wait. I see a distortion outside of me and inside me. To see that, there must be freedom. That freedom implies energy, and the seeing clears it. Now there is rational, sane thinking. What is the relationship of that to this space in the mind?

DAVID BOHM: That only arises when the space has cleared the thought. From then on it may be moving parallel to truth.

KRISHNAMURTI: Yes, that's what I want to find out. Is it parallel, or is there harmony between the two?

DAVID BOHM: In some way it is harmony. I wanted to say that in some sense thought is also that which is. Therefore thought, which is within that which is, is in harmony with the whole of that which is.

KRISHNAMURTI: Quite. I understand.

DAVID BOHM: Now if there is this harmony, that is also that which is.

KRISHNAMURTI: Can we put it this way for the moment? Thought is measure, time; that measurement can be distorted or rational. That's clear. So thought is a movement in the field of time. And, we say, truth is not related to that.

DAVID BOHM: In a sense, in one way. Truth does not depend on thought, but thought may depend on truth. Thought may be acted on by truth.

KRISHNAMURTI: Truth can act upon thought, that's understood. Now let's get it clear. Then what is the problem? Then they are all in the same field, aren't they, in the same space within the mind?

DAVID BOHM: Yes.

KRISHNAMURTI: Therefore there is no division. There is no division as thought and truth.

DAVID BOHM: The division is the result of thought which is not straight.

KRISHNAMURTI: That's right. So as it is in the same field...

DAVID BOHM: Therefore thought is also within truth – it moves in harmony with truth.

KRISHNAMURTI: Just a minute, I'm not quite sure. Thought, we said, is of time.

DAVID BOHM: Of time.

KRISHNAMURTI: Thought is time, measure, and all the rest of it. We said truth is not that. What is the relationship of thought to truth? When that question is put, your thought is looking to truth.

DAVID BOHM: Yes.

KRISHNAMURTI: And therefore it has no relationship. But when truth looks at thought, it says, 'I have a relationship', in the sense of – to use a quick phrase – 'I function in the field of time'.

DAVID BOHM: And that is the same as the field of reality, isn't it?

KRISHNAMURTI: I function in the field of reality. Now do they run parallel all the time or is there no division at all when truth is looking? It's only a division when thought...

DAVID BOHM: When thought tries to reflect truth within itself. I think that is where the trouble arises. It may be the whole trouble, that thought tries to reflect truth in itself, and calls that an independent reality.

KRISHNAMURTI: Yes, when thought reflects upon truth, then there is a division.

DAVID BOHM: Thought intrinsically divides itself from truth, but that is false because thought is only reflecting.

KRISHNAMURTI: Quite. But when truth regards reality, there is no division. We said when truth operates in the field of reality, it is operating with intelligence.

DAVID BOHM: Yes. Reality is a necessary field for truth to operate in. The difficulty is when thought starts, and tries to reflect on truth, and divides itself from truth. Therefore it produces the *notion* of reality and of the truth about that reality.

KRISHNAMURTI: And therefore it's divided and fragmented, yes.

DAVID BOHM: And also it gives this reality the significance of that which is, so it must distort. The basic thing that goes wrong is when reality is given the significance of that which is. If reality is simply an action, a function of intelligence, then it's all part of it, it's one.

KRISHNAMURTI: Yes. When intelligence operates in the field of reality, it is one, it doesn't divide.

DAVID BOHM: Reality is merely a field, it is not that which is, or an independent substance.

KRISHNAMURTI: This is something we have discovered.

DAVID BOHM: And then there is the space. The field of reality is in the space.

KRISHNAMURTI: Wait, that means thought is in the space.

DAVID BOHM: To explain it a little: when I start from the thought of reality, as that which is, then I think this thing is a substance which is just by itself, and here is another one, and they are separated by space. But if I look at it another way and I say, 'There is truth', the space acts, and reality is merely a function, it is not a set of independent substances. That's what I'm driving at – each one by itself, separate from all the others, is not that which is.

KRISHNAMURTI: Are you saying, sir, when truth operates in reality, then in that there is no division?

DAVID BOHM: There is no division because we don't think reality stands by itself and truth is somewhere else out there. Rather, reality is a function within the operation of truth.

KRISHNAMURTI: So truth has a need for reality.

DAVID BOHM: When the function is given the value of that which is, then it must become all-important, because that which is is all-important. And then the whole thing must distort.

KRISHNAMURTI: So you're telling me, 'Don't be concerned with truth, be concerned with reality and its distortions.'

DAVID BOHM: Yes, one has to observe them.

KRISHNAMURTI: 'Don't be concerned with truth, you don't know what it means. Be concerned only with reality and its distortions. Reality is thought and all the rest of it.' And you say to me, 'Be free of distortions, and to be free of distortions, just observe the distortions, don't resist them, just observe them. That observation needs freedom and that freedom and the observation will give you energy to push away the distortions. And the seeing of that distortion is the truth. So the truth is not something separate from seeing and doing, they are all one. And this is intelligence which operates in the field of reality without distortion.'

When I have freed myself from distortion, then truth is the seeing and the doing and the operation of that intelligence in the field of reality. That's all I know, actually. I have in my consciousness a great many distorting factors. Do I wipe them all out with one observation, or am I to take them one by one?

DAVID BOHM: You can't deal with them one by one.

KRISHNAMURTI: Therefore seeing is the whole. When you see the whole, that is the truth.

DAVID BOHM: That is the truth, to see the whole of the reality without distortion.

KRISHNAMURTI: To see that, the mind must have space.

DAVID BOHM: Could you say that the mind is not occupied with all...?

KRISHNAMURTI: Of course, occupation implies corruption.

DAVID BOHM: The word 'emptiness' means 'not occupied'.

KRISHNAMURTI: It is empty because it has no problems. The emptying of the mind of its content is meditation.

DAVID BOHM: There's just one point that occurred to me. It seems that something which comes close to the essence of this distortion is the tendency to take the whole field of reality as that which is.

KRISHNAMURTI: Sir, if the mind discards and puts away *all* distortion, what is the necessity of thought? Except as a function.

DAVID BOHM: As a rational function.

KRISHNAMURTI: That's all.

DAVID BOHM: Yes. I think many people feel that thought ought to be a rational function, but they can't make it so.

KRISHNAMURTI: If there is no controller of thought then it creates all kinds of distortions.

DAVID BOHM: Not if the truth is operating.

KRISHNAMURTI: That's it. Therefore thought itself is a distorting factor if truth is not operating.

DAVID BOHM: If truth is not operating, then thought moves in all sorts of fortuitous ways, like the wind and the waves. The waves come in and they go this way and that way. Whatever happens, thought will make it go all around and distort it.

KRISHNAMURTI: Would you say thought in itself is divisive, is in itself distorting, is creating distortions?

DAVID BOHM: Are you saying it necessarily does so? There are two possibilities. One is to say that thought without truth necessarily distorts; the other is to say that no matter what happens, thought is distorting. I don't think we want to say that thought inevitably distorts.

KRISHNAMURTI: No, the other.

DAVID BOHM: So we say thought without truth is a divisive process.

KRISHNAMURTI: That's right. Thought without that quality of seeing is a distorting factor.

Brockwood Park, 24 May 1975

2 Desire and goodness

DAVID BOHM: We have been saying that thought does not go straight, it tends to twist; and this is the major cause of the confusion in which mankind generally finds itself. It seems to me that desire may be what is behind this tendency of thought to become crooked. Perhaps we could begin by discussing desire.

KRISHNAMURTI: Why has desire become such an extraordinarily important thing in life?

DAVID BOHM: I looked up the word. It's based on a French word that originally meant 'something missing'. And its basic meaning is yearning, longing, craving and hankering. Words closely associated to desire are 'belief' and 'hope'. In hope, for example, there is the confident expectation that the desire will be realized. And I think belief is connected with it. What you believe is what you desire to be so. It's a source of crookedness, because you accept something as true just because you desire it to be so. The whole story of belief, hope and despair is in desire. Now the question is: what is it we long for and why do we long for it?

KRISHNAMURTI: Yes, what is the meaning of 'long for'?

DAVID BOHM: That's very ambiguous.

KRISHNAMURTI: Does one long for anything actual, or something abstract?

DAVID BOHM: It seems to me that in general one longs for something abstract.

KRISHNAMURTI: I might long for a car.

DAVID BOHM: Yes, but suppose that you long to end this state of society which is ugly and you hope to make it different.

KRISHNAMURTI: Yes. Is thought separate from desire?

DAVID BOHM: That's a question we have to go into, but in general I would say that thought and desire are the same.

KRISHNAMURTI: So would I.

DAVID BOHM: Usually we are caught in a kind of desire for that which is imagined.

KRISHNAMURTI: So it is part of thought.

DAVID BOHM: It is part of thought, but then you seem also to be describing something else, which is not part of thought. You start from perception.

KRISHNAMURTI: Not only perception. I see a car. I see the colour, the shape of the car, the ugliness of that particular car, and I don't want it, I wouldn't own it. That is a perception, a sensation.

DAVID BOHM: But sensation is also part of perception.

KRISHNAMURTI: You can't separate the two, but which is first, sensation or perception?

DAVID BOHM: I feel that perception is first. You can't have a sensation of something unless there is something to be seen.

KRISHNAMURTI: And then, how does desire arise from perception?

DAVID BOHM: Somehow thought and imagination come in. But you seem to say it's more direct than that.

KRISHNAMURTI: Does imagination come into it?

DAVID BOHM: In the form that desire usually takes, it does. Most of our desires are for things that are imagined; but I gave the example of the intense desire for a different state of society on the part of many people, which drives them very hard. I think that new state of society is imagined, isn't it?

KRISHNAMURTI: Let's see now. A group of us want to change the structure of society.

DAVID BOHM: Into something better, say.

KRISHNAMURTI: The desire is born out of perception of the state of society which actually is.

DAVID BOHM: Which is very ugly. So seeing or observing or thinking what the society now is, and hoping to change that, I imagine a better state.

KRISHNAMURTI: Is that part of desire?

DAVID BOHM: It seems so, at least at first sight. It seems that there is an intense desire for that imagined state.

KRISHNAMURTI: Or is it perception?

DAVID BOHM: How is that?

KRISHNAMURTI: I perceive the rottenness, or the corruption, or the malaise of this society. I see it. That perception drives me, not my desire to change society. My perception says this is ugly and that very perception is the action of the movement to change it. I don't know if I'm making myself clear.

DAVID BOHM: Yes, then there's a longing to change it.

KRISHNAMURTI: Is there a longing?

DAVID BOHM: If we say it's desire, it's implied.

KRISHNAMURTI: Desire? I'm just seeing.

DAVID BOHM: If we go back to the meaning of that word, something is missing. There is a longing for something that's missing.

KRISHNAMURTI: Or I perceive. That very perception, we said, is action. The perception of the society as it is is ugly – let's use that word for the moment. That very perception demands action.

DAVID BOHM: Yes, but we can't act immediately.

KRISHNAMURTI: The perception then begins to formulate what kind of action is to take place.

DAVID BOHM: That comes by thinking about it.

KRISHNAMURTI: Yes, of course. Is perception a part of desire?

DAVID BOHM: I should say it's not in the beginning, but as soon as it reaches the sense of ugliness or beauty, it's implicit. If you merely see the state of society without a sense that it is ugly or beautiful...

KRISHNAMURTI: No, perception itself is action. The ugliness of society is perceived. I won't even use the word 'ugly', because then we have to go into the contrary. Perception is the root of action. And that action may take time, and all the rest of it. Where does desire come into this? I don't see it.

DAVID BOHM: Well, why do you say that? What would you say to those people who want to change society?

KRISHNAMURTI: I would say, 'Is it your perception that is action? Or your prejudice, or desire to change society in order to achieve something else?'

DAVID BOHM: That is still a desire.

KRISHNAMURTI: That is desire. Is perception part of desire? I don't think it is.

DAVID BOHM: No. You have frequently said that there is perception, contact and sensation, and then that becomes desire.

KRISHNAMURTI: Yes, that is quite right. But once there is perception, where does desire come into it in carrying out that perception?

DAVID BOHM: In principle, if you could immediately carry it out there would be no need for the desire.

KRISHNAMURTI: Of course, that's one thing. But I can't carry it out immediately.

DAVID BOHM: Therefore you think something is missing. What I see should be this way, but I can't do it immediately.

KRISHNAMURTI: You perceive the actual – let's put it like this – actuality is perceived. In that actuality of perception, where does desire come in?

DR PARCHURE: Not in the actuality of perception.

KRISHNAMURTI: That's what I am saying.

DAVID BOHM: But we have to find out why it does come in.

KRISHNAMURTI: That's what I want to get at.

DAVID BOHM: Let us take something very simple. I perceive some object, like an apple. I would like to eat it and I just eat it – there's no problem of desire. It is there.

KRISHNAMURTI: Let's move a little further.

DAVID BOHM: On the other hand, if I can't get the apple, then there may come the problem of desire. I'm not saying it's right or wrong, but suppose that I perceive something which I can't get immediately, or which I don't know how to get. Then desire may arise. But it doesn't have to.

KRISHNAMURTI: It may arise because I want that apple, because I like the taste and so on. That's one thing. I perceive the actuality of society and I act – where does desire come in there?

DAVID BOHM: If you do act, desire doesn't come in, but you may feel that you don't know how to act.

KRISHNAMURTI: I may not know how to act, therefore I'll consult, talk.

DAVID BOHM: While you are consulting you may become discouraged.

KRISHNAMURTI: My perception is so clear it cannot be discouraged.

DAVID BOHM: That may be so, but I am describing what generally happens. Let's say I perceive the falseness and rottenness of society, and I consider how to change it. I talk with people and so on, but after a while I begin to see that it doesn't change all that easily. Perhaps at some stage I may begin to feel it doesn't look possible at all. But then may come a longing to change it nevertheless.

KRISHNAMURTI: No, if I see it is not possible to change it, then it's finished. Then that's it.

DAVID BOHM: Yes, but why is it that people don't accept that? I'm just describing what is the general experience. On seeing that this thing is not possible, there is a longing for that which is not possible. And that is the form of desire that is always frustrated, which creates all these problems.

KRISHNAMURTI: Yes.

DAVID BOHM: Now, on the other hand, you can't say people should accept that society will go on being false forever.

KRISHNAMURTI: Sir, is it perception that's driving them, or that they have never perceived and only desire is operating?

DAVID BOHM: That may be, but it seems that the desire itself was born of perception, at least what they think was perception. But then the question is, where did desire actually originate?

KRISHNAMURTI: That's a different matter.

DAVID BOHM: It seems mysterious why there should be this desire there.

KRISHNAMURTI: No. I see that car, I'd like to own it, I associate that car with pleasure.

DAVID BOHM: It would only be possible to get caught in that if, at some stage, perception failed.

KRISHNAMURTI: I don't quite follow.

DAVID BOHM: Well, you see, if you say, 'I'd like to own the car', there's still no problem unless you have this intense longing, which is desire, which drives you.

KRISHNAMURTI: I see.

DAVID BOHM: You could say, 'I'd like to own the car; if it's possible, I'll own it, if it's not, I won't.'

KRISHNAMURTI: I won't, that's simple. There's no problem.

DAVID BOHM: But that is not usually what is meant by desire.

KRISHNAMURTI: Desire means longing for.

DAVID BOHM: Longing for what you cannot get. Whether you can get it or not, you long for it.

KRISHNAMURTI: You see, I don't function that way.

DAVID BOHM: We have to understand this function, because it seems to be the general function.

KRISHNAMURTI: That is the general function, I agree.

DAVID BOHM: First of all, it's not clear to me why it should be there. Rationally, there's no reason for it. But as far as one can see, it is still there, very powerful, all over the world.

KRISHNAMURTI: Is desire based on sensation, imagination, an imagined pleasure one is going to get?

DAVID BOHM: Yes, I think it's based on the imagination of not merely a pleasure, but of beauty, or even of what is good. People generally desire things which are regarded as beautiful. Take things like gold or precious stones, which have very little value in themselves. People have attached value to them because of their eternal beauty. Therefore they are ready to do anything for such things.

KRISHNAMURTI: Desire for power, position.

DAVID BOHM: It's the same thing.

KRISHNAMURTI: The same thing. How does it arise? Is that the question?

DAVID BOHM: Yes, how does it arise and what is the meaning of it?

KRISHNAMURTI: How does it arise? I see you driving in a big car, or you, the politician, in a big position, and I want that, I'd like to have that.

DAVID BOHM: It's not clear why I drive myself to such lengths.

KRISHNAMURTI: It gives me tremendous pleasure.

DAVID BOHM: Yes, but then, why do I want the pleasure? Unless I've been confusing this pleasure with something else, which would be of tremendous value.

KRISHNAMURTI: Is pleasure the only thing I know?

DAVID BOHM: But I know a lot of things, I know all sorts of things.

KRISHNAMURTI: Or is it that I live such a superficial life? My education is superficial and pleasure is superficial and so I long for that.

DAVID BOHM: But it must seem that it's not superficial, or it wouldn't be worth longing for. I don't think anybody longs for something he recognizes to be superficial.

KRISHNAMURTI: No, if I recognize pleasure as superficial, there's no longing.

DAVID BOHM: But somehow there's a feeling that pleasure is something else, something very significant, very deep. Or at least that it may be.

KRISHNAMURTI: Of course it may look like that, but is it actually?

DAVID BOHM: It isn't actually, but why does it look that way?

KRISHNAMURTI: Why am I deceived by thinking pleasure is very deep?

DAVID BOHM: Yes.

KRISHNAMURTI: Sir, is pleasure one of the factors of covering my emptiness?

DAVID BOHM: It may be. I think that pleasure helps create the impression of some sort of full, harmonious, beautiful life.

KRISHNAMURTI: Is pleasure associated with beauty?

DAVID BOHM: I think it is. In general the very fact that the word 'love' is connected with desire, also with beauty, would suggest that pleasure and beauty are associated. People generally expect that a beautiful thing will give pleasurable experiences.

KRISHNAMURTI: Yes, I understand that. I see something very beautiful – where does pleasure arise in that? I'd like to own it, I'd like to possess it.

DAVID BOHM: I'd like to have it forever; I'd like the experience to be repeated somehow.

KRISHNAMURTI: Yes, I'd like to have it forever. Why do I do this?

DAVID BOHM: Because of a kind of fear that I'll be without it.

KRISHNAMURTI: Is it in myself – that I'm not beautiful?

DAVID BOHM: That may be part of it. A sense of not having contact with beauty in myself and therefore wanting something other.

KRISHNAMURTI: So is beauty out there and therefore I want it?

DAVID BOHM: It's both. The dictionary says beauty is not merely the quality of the thing but the quality of the person. In other words, it's both the quality of the thing and the quality of the sensation. In some sense there is no division of the observer and the observed. But suppose I have no beauty, no contact with beauty, but by seeing a thing I create a sense of the beauty of it in me.

KRISHNAMURTI: Yes, I understand that.

DAVID BOHM: And then, suppose the thing has gone. So I'm back in the previous state. Then I begin to long for that experience again.

KRISHNAMURTI: So what is the problem, sir?

DAVID BOHM: I think that the question really is to understand this process of desire, because without understanding it I don't think the confusion around thought will end. On the one side is the desire and on the other side there's what we've been discussing, truth and reality and so on. Desire is on the side of feeling. Once confusion arises in desire then it drives the whole mind into crookedness, into imagining that everything is or can be as one desires it to be.

KRISHNAMURTI: Would you say desire is in the field of reality?

DAVID BOHM: Yes, it seems that it is in the field of reality, but it presents itself in some way as not being in the field. It presents itself as apparently a way to truth.

KRISHNAMURTI: Can I desire truth?

DAVID BOHM: That's something else. It would seem I could desire truth; at the very least I could desire beauty or goodness. It's generally accepted that you could have a desire for the good or the beautiful or the true, at least in the common usage of language.

KRISHNAMURTI: I am questioning that. Is beauty in the realm of reality?

DAVID BOHM: Or is the good in the realm of reality? Because I think I should say that most people regard good and beauty as almost equivalent.

KRISHNAMURTI: Synonymous. Are beauty, love and goodness in the field of reality, created by thought, and something I long to get?

DAVID BOHM: If they are in the field of reality, then I could reasonably long to get them.

KRISHNAMURTI: That's it. And are that goodness, beauty and love actually in the field of reality?

DAVID BOHM: No.

KRISHNAMURTI: But desire is in the field of reality.

DAVID BOHM: Yes, desire is a movement in the field of reality and it tries to project into that field something which should properly be outside of it.

KRISHNAMURTI: Yes. That which is projected is actually part of reality, but one doesn't recognize that.

DAVID BOHM: That's right. You see that's why there is always a contradiction in desire.

KRISHNAMURTI: Of course, that's right.

DAVID BOHM: Because you project something that seems to be beyond the field of reality, and even when you achieve what you think you wanted, you feel this is not all that you wanted. Something is still sensed as missing, in the reality that you have achieved.

KRISHNAMURTI: Right. So, is beauty in the field of reality at all?

DAVID BOHM: No, I think it's clear it's not.

KRISHNAMURTI: Obviously not. Then, as *longing for beauty* is in the field of reality, it is a movement of thought projecting beauty and longing for it. Could we ask, what is beauty or goodness which is not in the field of reality?

DAVID BOHM: I'm puzzled about beauty, which seems rather mysterious in some ways. Let us say there is an object – a tree – in the field of reality, which is beautiful. But it is not beauty. In other words, beauty is not in the field of reality, it's the essence.

KRISHNAMURTI: Quite. I would say beauty is not in the field of reality.

DAVID BOHM: Yes, but the tree is in the field of reality.

KRISHNAMURTI: The tree *is*, it is.

DAVID BOHM: That's right. Then we have to get it clear, because in the ordinary use of language we would say the tree is real.

KRISHNAMURTI: Yes, quite.

DAVID BOHM: For example, if you were a lumberman, you would treat it as a reality.

KRISHNAMURTI: Of course. But what is, is beautiful.

DAVID BOHM: Yes, all right, but then we are liable to fall into a difficulty of language, if we say that the tree is not real, but that it *is*. The tree is that which is, but it's not real.

KRISHNAMURTI: Yes, put it that way.

DAVID BOHM: But that is such a violation of the ordinary use of language.

KRISHNAMURTI: The tree, as we generally accept it, is a reality. But that which is, we say, is truth. And I, looking at the tree, bring it into the field of reality by thinking about it.

DAVID BOHM: Also acting on it as a real thing.

KRISHNAMURTI: Yes, as a carpenter.

Now let us get it clear. We say, goodness is not in the field of reality.

DAVID BOHM: It may act there, but in essence it is not there.

KRISHNAMURTI: In essence it is not in the field of reality. Good works, good behaviour, good taste, good food, good thoughts, are all in the field of reality. But *goodness*, the essence of it, is not.

DAVID BOHM: In the conference with the scientists you mentioned some sort of universal energy, that is self-sustaining and orderly.

KRISHNAMURTI: Yes, non-contradictory.

DAVID BOHM: So it is a kind of self-sustaining energy of cosmic significance, not belonging to any particular thing or set of things.

KRISHNAMURTI: Yes.

DAVID BOHM: Now is this the energy of that which is? Is that what you mean to say?

KRISHNAMURTI: Let's go into this carefully.

DAVID BOHM: This idea has in fact arisen in many contexts, even in physics. I won't go into it now, but a rather similar idea has been suggested in physics, that there is an energy in empty space which is in perfect order.

KRISHNAMURTI: Yes, I agree, which is in perfect order.

Sir, reality is a thing. Truth is not a thing, therefore it is nothing. The thing creates energy...

DAVID BOHM: A kind of energy.

KRISHNAMURTI: One kind of energy.

DAVID BOHM: Limited energy.

KRISHNAMURTI: The not-a-thing, which is empty, is unlimited.

DAVID BOHM: It has unlimited energy. What you imply is that that unlimited energy is self-sustaining, it doesn't depend on any thing.

KRISHNAMURTI: It doesn't depend. This depends, the other doesn't.

DAVID BOHM: And ultimately even this may depend on that. Is that a possibility, that the thing ultimately depends on the unlimited, on that?

KRISHNAMURTI: Of course. That is what is being said. But then we're caught in a trap, which is: God is in us, that supreme energy is in man.

DAVID BOHM: No, let's try to put it differently. The problem was related to the question raised in the conference of scientists as to whether this energy and the energy of thought...

KRISHNAMURTI: Is one thing.

DAVID BOHM: Is it all one energy which is being used wrongly? We never quite settled the question. I think it's similar to ask if there is one energy which makes the emptiness and the things or are there two energies?

KRISHNAMURTI: There is only one energy. There is only one energy which is used in reality and therefore is destructible, perverted, deteriorating, degenerating and all the rest of it. That same energy is nothingness, nothingness being death. Yes, sir?

DAVID BOHM: Right.

KRISHNAMURTI: I think – I am just hesitating to put it forth – that the energy born of nothingness is nevertheless different from the other.

DAVID BOHM: But is there some unity, some connection?

KRISHNAMURTI: I think there is a one-way connection – that is, from nothingness to thing; but from thing to nothingness is not possible. So, now let's go on, slowly. Is the energy of nothingness different from the energy of thing? For the moment, I see that it is different, different in the sense of being dissimilar.

DAVID BOHM: They are dissimilar, yes, that's one meaning of 'different'. It allows for a one-way relationship.

KRISHNAMURTI: Or are they both the same? One is in the field of reality and therefore misused, deteriorating and all the rest of it, and the other is endless, it is not limited.

DAVID BOHM: In other words, instead of saying there are two, we say there is one which is infinite, but the infinite includes the finite, does not exclude it. That is one proposal.

KRISHNAMURTI: The other proposal is, there is no relationship from the thing to nothingness.

DAVID BOHM: No, that's the same in both proposals. If you say it is infinite and contains the finite, therefore the infinite is related towards the finite, but it doesn't mean the finite can do anything to the infinite.

KRISHNAMURTI: Quite. But I see it as being different.

DAVID BOHM: All right.

KRISHNAMURTI: We said the nothingness is death, which means total ending. Thought in the world of reality has never an ending. Thought creates its own energy. Are they both the same thing, from the same source? In one, human beings degenerate that energy, and the source is polluted in the world of reality. It is the same energy in the world of truth. Is that it? You misuse electricity, and somebody else doesn't misuse it. It is all electricity. Or is that energy which is of nothingness totally different, dissimilar?

Let's put it this way, sir: from the field of reality can there be a movement to truth?

DAVID BOHM: No.

KRISHNAMURTI: No. Why?

DAVID BOHM: Because the field of reality is conditioned, it's made of things.

KRISHNAMURTI: So, as it cannot, as it has no relationship to truth, then truth cannot act in the world of reality. Then there's no connection.

DAVID BOHM: We have said that there is a one-way connection.

KRISHNAMURTI: Therefore it is not an interacting relationship.

DAVID BOHM: No, it's not a mutual relationship, it's one way. Perhaps you could say truth acts in reality through death; that is, through ending the false, for example.

KRISHNAMURTI: Yes. We go back to the same thing. Thought can be ended, obviously, one can see that. Is that ending of thought the same as 'not a thing'?

DAVID BOHM: Well.

KRISHNAMURTI: No, sir, I think this is right. There are two separate energies. The energy of no thing is totally different from the other.

DAVID BOHM: But then you haven't explained why there can be a relationship in which that no thing operates in the field of thought or reality.

KRISHNAMURTI: It cannot operate because it's everything.

DAVID BOHM: Yes, but this means that it includes the field of reality.

KRISHNAMURTI: No.

DAVID BOHM: Then what do you mean by saying every *thing*? Doesn't this include whatever *things* are in the field of reality?

KRISHNAMURTI: One must be careful here. We say nothingness means ending; that is, not a thing. In the world of reality, ending means continuation in a different form. Now this – truth – has no continuity; *that* has a continuity.

DAVID BOHM: Yes, all right, that difference we can see.

KRISHNAMURTI: That has a movement in time, this has no movement in time. Are they the same movement?

DAVID BOHM: Is time a sort of a small movement within the infinite?

KRISHNAMURTI: Quite.

DAVID BOHM: Because you did use the analogy, in the scientists' conference, of some small area inside a big space. Now, do you want to look at time that way?

KRISHNAMURTI: Yes, I see that. No, I still feel in my blood, this is totally different.

DAVID BOHM: Totally different, yes.

KRISHNAMURTI: Let's put it round this way, sir. In the field of reality, love has a different meaning – there is jealousy and so on.

DAVID BOHM: That's when it's trapped in there, but I'm suggesting that love can act in the field of reality in a clear way.

KRISHNAMURTI: Yes, love can act in the world of reality, but the love in reality is not *love*.

DAVID BOHM: It's desire.

KRISHNAMURTI: Desire and all the rest of it. We're getting slowly back.

DAVID BOHM: Therefore, if it's trapped in there, love in the field of reality is not *love*.

KRISHNAMURTI: So the love in nothingness can act in the world of reality, but it can never be polluted in the field of reality, therefore it is something entirely original.

Sir, could we begin the other way round? We said death is ending and that which has a continuity can never be created. That which has a movement, in the time sense, has no ending. And we said death, inward death, is the ending of everything, *every thing*. There is no relationship between the two. I would like to think that I can use the action of truth in the world of reality.

DAVID BOHM: We have nevertheless been saying so far that truth does act in reality.

KRISHNAMURTI: Now is that so? Can it? It has no movement, how can not-a-thing act in reality? Reality is a thing.

Sir, would you put it this way? Can a mind that has no measure, that is not living in the world of measure, operate in the world of measure?

DAVID BOHM: What does operate then?

KRISHNAMURTI: Only measure.

DAVID BOHM: Measure operates in the world of measure, but this mind operates to see the falseness in that measure. Because I see I make the measurement and it is wrong, then...

KRISHNAMURTI: Then I alter the measurement.

DAVID BOHM: But before I alter it, I have to see that it is false. Now isn't that the operation of truth?

KRISHNAMURTI: No. I measure the length of the table and I see it doesn't fit into the room.

DAVID BOHM: Yes, all right, but how do I see it? If the mind is operating clearly it will see that, otherwise it may become confused and not see it.

KRISHNAMURTI: Yes, that's clear. If I measure properly with a tape measure, and stick to that, then it's right. But it's still in the world of measurement.

DAVID BOHM: Yes, measurement operates in the world of measurement. Thought is part of measurement. But it's important that thought should be clear, free of confusion, free of falseness. At present, through desire and through other factors, thought twists and becomes false. Now, what is the difference between the mind in which thought is crooked and the one in which thought is not crooked?

KRISHNAMURTI: Can't my crookedness be seen in the world of reality?

DAVID BOHM: No, it's the truth of it that's seen – the truth of the world of reality. The truth of the world of reality is that it is false and crooked.

KRISHNAMURTI: Yes. Sir, may we say this: the world of reality is measurement – let's stick to that for the moment – and that measurement may be false or true?

DAVID BOHM: Yes, it may be *correct*. I would rather not say *true*.

KRISHNAMURTI: Let's put it that way – that measurement may be false or correct in the field of reality. Now, in nothingness there is no measurement. Now what is the relationship between the two? This has measurement, that has no measurement.

DAVID BOHM: Yes, but what is it that sees whether the measurement is fitting? If the measurement is false, there is contradiction. Now what is it that sees the contradiction? The world of measure cannot have any criteria in it to guarantee correctness. Something beyond it is needed.

KRISHNAMURTI: Quite. But if my measurement is incorrect there is disturbance.

DAVID BOHM: Yes, but then because my reality is crooked, I may suppress awareness of that disturbance.

KRISHNAMURTI: Yes, but it is still in that area.

DAVID BOHM: It is in that area, but what is it that sees that there is disturbance in that area?

KRISHNAMURTI: I perceive that I am disturbed.

DAVID BOHM: Yes, but many people don't perceive.

KRISHNAMURTI: Because they're insensitive, they are not aware, they are not conscious. But it is still there.

DAVID BOHM: Yes, then why not? Why are they not conscious?

KRISHNAMURTI: Because of education, of ten different reasons. There is measurement in reality, false measurement and correct measurement. Let's stick to that for the moment. And as you say, who perceives the false and the correct? Who is the entity that sees in the world of reality the false and the correct? It is still the same mind which has measured.

DAVID BOHM: Yes, but then there's no meaning to it, because this may be false at the next step.

KRISHNAMURTI: Of course.

DAVID BOHM: But still, it seems there is some meaning to a thing being correct.

KRISHNAMURTI: Yes, it fits, it's suitable, it's happy, it is convenient, it is still *there* in that field. I must stick to it. It is still there.

DAVID BOHM: Yes, it's still in that field, but in that field there is no way to guarantee...

KRISHNAMURTI: Pure correctness.

DAVID BOHM: It still seems to me that there must be some perception beyond that field.

KRISHNAMURTI: Why? Why should there be some other perception except that? You can only say there is some other perception when there is actually nothingness. Is that nothingness a hypothesis, a theory, a verbal structure, or truth? If it is a verbal structure, it is still in the world of reality.

DAVID BOHM: Well, naturally, if it's a verbal structure, it won't change.

KRISHNAMURTI: If it is still a theory, a hypothesis, a thing thought out, it is still *there*. *Here*, we say, there is no entrance for thought, therefore it is nothing. And we're asking: is there a relationship between the two? That's the central point we're trying to find out. If I say there is a relationship between this and that, then what takes place? I endeavour, struggle, to reach that. Therefore I imagine I have a relationship to that, either in theory, in the hypothesis, or by hoping, which is desire. I'm caught in desire and hope, imagining I have a relationship with that. Why do I do it? Because I want something that's permanent, something that can never be hurt, something that is not ending, beginning, suffering, all that. So I project as an ideal, or an imagination, or a hope, or a desire, that there is that. When I project from this to that, whatever the projection is, that becomes unreal, imaginary, it is a fantasy.

Now if there is *actually* nothingness – not in theory – then where is the connection between the two? In dying to reality – it sounds absurd – only then is there nothingness. 'Dying to reality' means dying to all the things thought has created. It means dying to all the things of measurement, of movement, of time.

I know nothing about nothingness. I can't even imagine it. I don't know what it is, I'm not concerned with it, I'm only concerned with *this* – I live in *this*. And here I'm always caught between the false and the correct, between false measurement and correct measurement, and I'm adjusting myself always between the two. Or I am pursuing the one and rejecting the other. But it is still here. And do I see totally that desire has no end, hope has no end, struggle has no end if I live here?

I don't know anything about nothingness, that's all your invention. You may know what nothingness is – I shut my eyes to that – I only know *this* and my desire is not to enter that, but to be free of *this*.

DAVID BOHM: If it's a desire, it's still the same, isn't it?

KRISHNAMURTI: Yes, I'm saying my desire, my hope, my longing, is all from this. So I'm still exercising thought; therefore I'm still caught in the trap of trying to get to that. So you tell me to end thinking – but not because I want to get that. I *can* end it, but is such ending different from this?

DAVID BOHM: What do you mean? What is different?

KRISHNAMURTI: I can end thought by persuasion, by practice.

DAVID BOHM: That's still the same process.

KRISHNAMURTI: Of course. I feel I can end it.

DAVID BOHM: Yes, but that would still be the same.

KRISHNAMURTI: Therefore you'd still be there. Is there an ending here without a motive?

DAVID BOHM: Well, it seems you've brought in nothingness implicitly, by saying 'no motive'.

KRISHNAMURTI: So if I see the thing completely, there is an ending. Then this is that, then it is nothing. But I think it is a wrong question on my part to ask whether there is a relationship between the two. At least *I* won't ask it because I only know this.

As I only know this, my energy is limited to this, corrupted, perverted, distorted, neurotic, pathological, everything is that. And a man who says, 'There is nothingness' just says it; he doesn't relate this to that, he says, 'There is nothingness'. How will you catch him? He doesn't say, 'In nothingness everything is'. He sees the danger of that and says, 'I won't say this, there is only nothingness'. And another says, 'What's the use of that? It's not marketable, it doesn't relieve my pain, my agony – keep it to yourself.'

DAVID BOHM: Basically you're saying that we have to approach the thing with a right question that doesn't presuppose something wrong. But whatever may be right about nothingness, you can't properly and consistently say it from the starting-point, when you are in reality.

KRISHNAMURTI: That's right. Therefore the energy of nothingness is something quite different from this. And he says, 'Don't bother about it, look at reality and get out of it. Don't bother about the other. Don't bring the cosmos into the limited.'

DAVID BOHM: But you did bring it in during the conference with the scientists.

KRISHNAMURTI: I brought it in because I wanted them to know that something of that kind exists, not only all these little things. They may reject it. And you come along and say to me, 'There is a state of nothingness.' You say that, and it is tremendously true to you. And it means dying, all that, not a thing in one's mind. I hear that, because you have said it. I have the feeling that it's true, because of the very way you are saying it, because of your very presence; you are very sane, your very world *has* that. And I want to enter into it. But you say, 'Go to hell, you can't do it.' I think that's right, otherwise we get caught in the ancient trap of 'God is here', 'Truth is in reality', and all the rest of it.

Does this answer, sir, that beauty, goodness, truth – the purity of it – is in nothingness? But the good, the beautiful, the correct, are all in the field of reality, which is different from the other. I think that's right.

DAVID BOHM: I think that one has a general expectation that the state of nothingness would not produce a man who acted from evil.

KRISHNAMURTI: Don't you see?

DAVID BOHM: Yes, I know, but I'm just saying this.

KRISHNAMURTI: That's a wrong question.

DAVID BOHM: But we have to look at the question, in the sense that it is one which is present in us, in our background, in our tradition throughout the whole world. It's part of the tradition that a man who acts from the nothingness or from God, whatever people call it, would not do evil things.

KRISHNAMURTI: Look, sir, there is, after all, in the Jewish and in the Hindu world – not in the Christian – the nameless, the immeasurable. I've lived *here*, and name 'Him' all the time. And 'He' doesn't even recognize the name. I think that's true. So my only concern is here. Do I see the totality of this? If I see it, I'm out.

Sir, that holds true, I'll stick to it.

Therefore there is no relationship between the two. For a man who experiences death – I won't use the word 'experiences' – a man who dies – not under anaesthesia in an operation, or by accident, disease, or old age – but dies because he is alive, active, there is a total ending; he has ended. The ending in reality is quite different, therefore there's no relationship.

Right, I stick to this. I'm clear. I fight all the scientists on that!

Sir, the love that exists in reality is one thing. That same word cannot be applied here. You can call it 'compassion', you can call it something else, but it's not the same word, the same content of that word.

DAVID BOHM: The other day we were discussing love as movement in relationship, but that would seem at first sight to be the field of reality, since relationship is in that field.

KRISHNAMURTI: Yes, it's still in that field now. But nothingness is something entirely different. My relationship here is a movement in time, in change, in breaking down one medium into another medium and so on. When I see the totality of that relationship, actually perceive it in the sense that the perceiver and the perceived are one, and there is no perceiver but only perception, that's the ending of the whole of that field.

Then I ask, 'What is relationship when all that has ended?' He says, 'Do that first, I'll answer afterwards.' He has climbed Everest and I haven't. He can describe to me the beauty of that climb, but I'm still in the valley. And I long to have that vision of what he has seen. My desire is for that. My desire is from the description, not from going up there.

I have no desire when I go climbing, in the climbing there is no desire. But in the attempt to achieve the description of what he has seen, there is desire. Right, sir, I think that says it. I think that's right. We are caught in description and are not actually climbing.

Brockwood Park, 14 June 1975

3   Beyond attention and awareness

DAVID BOHM: Over the years we have seen that thought moves in inevitable contradiction from one sphere to another. We have said, let's try to keep thought in its place, where it is technically efficient, and so on. But then one discovers that thought cannot stay in its place.

KRISHNAMURTI: Are we saying, sir, that thought, being in itself contradictory, when it tries to put order into that contradiction it creates further disorder; and that thought can never have its right place?

DAVID BOHM: Yes, even if we were able to start out entirely fresh, we would come to the same thing.

KRISHNAMURTI: Yes. Then, we are asking, is there an energy which will function without becoming crooked? Is that it?

DAVID BOHM: Yes. Because unless there is that, we must return to thought.

KRISHNAMURTI: So we are asking if thought can be an instrument that can discover anything which is not crooked.

We've come to the point, now, where we said that thought, being contradictory in its very nature, can resolve one contradiction and create another contradiction. And it keeps on repeating this, hoping thereby to come to a certain point when thought itself sees its absurdity. Then, seeing its absurdity, thought invents, or conceives, a new pattern. But it is still thought. So we have reached that point and we see that the movement of thought must always be contradictory, self-perpetuating and so on. Can that thought end, and a new energy operate in the field of reality which does not bring about contradiction in that field?

DAVID BOHM: On the intellectual side we see contradiction, and on the other side we have a feeling it comes through desire. It comes to the same thing.

KRISHNAMURTI: Sir, when we use the word 'desire', we use it in the sense of feeling, demanding, longing, clinging to, seeking ultimate pleasure in different forms – the highest and the lowest, and so on. Surely all that is in the field of thought? Desire is one of the arms of thought, if we can put it that way.

DAVID BOHM: Yes, it's thought producing feeling.

KRISHNAMURTI: Would there be desire, would there be a feeling, if thought didn't enter into that area?

DAVID BOHM: That's the question. In general in our culture it's accepted that there would be. But on the other hand, if it were not identified by thought as a certain kind of feeling, it's hard to say what it would be.

KRISHNAMURTI: Quite. I desire this house, or I desire something else. In that very desire is included the longing for that which thought has created. I want the image which thought has created as pleasurable. I want that pleasure. I don't think there is a difference between desire and thought.

DAVID BOHM: Yes, and the contradiction in desire comes in the same way. Just as there is inherently a contradiction in thought, so there is inherently a contradiction in desire.

KRISHNAMURTI: When I am young, I desire a woman; later, I desire a house. I change the objects of desire.

DAVID BOHM: That's the contradiction.

KRISHNAMURTI: But desire remains.

DAVID BOHM: Desire remains, but its object is always contradictory. It won't stay with an object. When you get it then there is another desire. It is the same as thought which will move from one thing to another.

KRISHNAMURTI: That is so. I think that's clear.

We said, desire is in its very nature contradictory, though it appears that the desire for objects may change. But in essence desire is contradictory, as thought is contradictory. So now we say, is there an energy which operates in the field of reality without becoming crooked?

You see, when I have discussed with Indian scholars and others, they have said this energy is divine – I'm using their words – and therefore it can never operate in the field of reality. If it does, it can never become contradictory. They presuppose, or imagine, there is an energy which is unconditioned, which is Brahman, God, or whatever it is. If we can erase from our minds that process of invention or imagining – as we must, if we really want to find out – then what have we? Then we have only thought, and desire in its essence, crooked in operation, and the result is contradictory, everlastingly. We know nothing else. I think that would be a sane position to take; at least I like to start that way.

I know nothing other than this crooked nature of thought, and desire which clings and changes its object of longing. I am aware of my consciousness, and in that consciousness all movement is thought and desire. That consciousness, because it is in constant movement, has never found an energy which is not contradictory, which is not produced by desire and thought. That is all I know. Then my problem is: can thought ever see its own movement and the futility of its own movement? 'Futile' in the sense of contradictory, conflicting. Can thought see totally its movement in consciousness? Can it see it as a whole?

DAVID BOHM: One can see difficulties there. Why it looks perhaps impossible is because ordinarily we think about something, and that very thought separates the thing we think about from the thought. As soon as we begin to say 'I am that thing that I think about', then it seems thought cannot be sustained.

KRISHNAMURTI: Yes, let's move from there. If my consciousness is myself, there is no separation between myself and the content of my consciousness, the content is me. I see that. Is that seeing within the field of consciousness, or outside it? When I say 'I see the contradictory nature of thought', is it a verbal perception, an intellectual comprehension, or is it actual perception? Is it an actuality? Let's put it that way. Or do I imagine that I see, or do I think I see, or is it that I desire to see and therefore I see? Is seeing, observing, perceiving, and so on, a movement of thought? If it is, then I don't see.

Then, when does the mind say 'I see'?

DAVID BOHM: When the movement of thought stops.

KRISHNAMURTI: Obviously. And what made it stop? How has that come about?

DAVID BOHM: Through seeing the contradiction, or the absurdity.

KRISHNAMURTI: Yes, but when you say contradiction and absurdity, is thought seeing, or does it imagine it's seeing?

DAVID BOHM: No, there is attention to what thought is doing, to the actuality.

KRISHNAMURTI: Yes, the actual is being seen. The actual which is the creation of thought. Desire is created by the movement of thought. That's the actual. And who is it that sees it? How does it happen?

DAVID BOHM: Well, there is nobody that sees it.

DR PARCHURE: It seems that attention is the thing that sees.

KRISHNAMURTI: I don't want to go back, I want to start anew.

I have a problem. Dr Bohm has shown me that thought is ever-lastingly moving from pattern to pattern as contradictory desires. When thought does that, there can be no solution or ending to that. And he says, there is no ending to sorrow, confusion, misery, conflict. I listen to him because he is telling me something serious. I am paying attention to it. I respect what he is saying, and at a given moment I see it. What do I see? The verbal pattern? I hear the verbal description and therefore have I caught the colour of the painting of the words? Or is it an intellectual grasp of what is being said, or has it nothing to do with any of that, but is only perception?

I have listened. To me it seems logical, sane and actual, that is all. And then at some moment I say, 'I see the whole of it' – not the fragments put together, but the whole movement of desire, thought, contradiction, the movement from pattern to pattern, the excuses. I see it completely as a whole; and my action of seeing it as a whole is totally different from thought/action.

I am asking you, how does this happen?

DAVID BOHM: It's not clear what you mean by 'how'. You see, when I was looking at it and I saw that thought could not be made straight, it seemed I couldn't describe what happened, but then at that moment I was no longer interested in trying to make thought straight, so I thought that this was seeing.

KRISHNAMURTI: Yes. Are you asking if thought sees itself in movement and contradiction?

DAVID BOHM: I am saying that when there is seeing, then this whole movement of contradiction no longer continues.

KRISHNAMURTI: Does thought see itself?

DAVID BOHM: No, it does not see itself. It seems to me in some vague sense that there is a bigger movement, or space.

KRISHNAMURTI: That may be imagined by thought.

DAVID BOHM: It may be imagined, yes.

KRISHNAMURTI: The scientists have said there is cosmic energy. I don't know anything about it. All that I know is this: having listened with attention, with respect, with care, suddenly I say, 'Yes, I see, I understand the whole of it, you don't have to talk any more about it.' What brought this about? If you say 'attention', that implies that there is no centre – centre as thought – which has created the 'me' and the 'not me' and all the rest of it.

Does this seeing come about when there is attention, which implies that there is no centre which thought has made and therefore I receive everything without twisting it?

DAVID BOHM: When thought makes the centre, that starts the twisting – is that what you are implying?

KRISHNAMURTI: Yes.

DAVID BOHM: But is there thought without a centre? Can there be thought before there is a centre? Is thought within the centre, or are thought and the centre more or less the same domain?

KRISHNAMURTI: Yes, the same domain.

DAVID BOHM: The weakness of thought is that thought inevitably separates itself from what it thinks about. It creates an imaginary other, which it calls the object – which is still really thought.

Let's say I'm thinking about the image of a tree. Now that which I am thinking about seems to be separated from me. It seems the image is over there somewhere and I am here. Therefore it seems that I have created two images, one is the tree and the other is me.

KRISHNAMURTI: That's right. The 'me' is the image which thought has created. There is the thinking about the tree and the thinking which has created an image in the mind as the 'me'.

DAVID BOHM: Yes, but it seems that thought presents those two as separate, when in fact it's one thought.

KRISHNAMURTI: Yes, that's one thought.

DAVID BOHM: Now, it would seem from what you say that there is no thought without the centre.

KRISHNAMURTI: That is the point, that's right.

DAVID BOHM: Well if some energy could take place without the centre, then we wouldn't have this problem.

KRISHNAMURTI: Yes, that's right.

Now, is the seeing within the field of consciousness? That means, seeing must have space, and is there a space which is not touched by thought in consciousness, and therefore from that space arises the total comprehension?

DAVID BOHM: Yes, but it's part of consciousness.

KRISHNAMURTI: Yes, that's it. It's part of the content of consciousness which has been conditioned by religion and so on. Then where does this seeing take place?

DAVID BOHM: In the case you were discussing, when the space is part of consciousness?

KRISHNAMURTI: Yes. I see that space is part of this consciousness and therefore it is still within the field of contradiction, still within the field of desire, in the field of reality which thought has created. I see that. But is there a perception, a seeing as a whole, outside it? And if there is an outside seeing – if I can use that word – then thought, or the centre which thought has created, with its periphery, and all that, comes to an end. Seeing is the ending of thought. Would you say that?

DAVID BOHM: Yes.

KRISHNAMURTI: Perception is not a movement of thought.

DAVID BOHM: When you perceive a contradiction, then thought stops.

KRISHNAMURTI: Yes. You see the truth outside the field of consciousness; truth is not within the field of consciousness. If it were, it would be reality and so on. Truth would still be contradictory if it were within that field. It would be your truth, my truth, his truth. If it is not in that field, it is truth. And because you see it, your action in the field of reality is never crooked. Right?

DAVID BOHM: Yes. Is it possible that you might fall back into contradiction?

KRISHNAMURTI: Never, if I see truth.

DAVID BOHM: Just once is enough?

KRISHNAMURTI: Absolutely. If there is a perception of truth, how can you go back into something which is not truth?

DAVID BOHM: But then, how do you come to make mistakes?

KRISHNAMURTI: We are saying truth cannot make a 'mistake' – in quotes.

DAVID BOHM: It can do things wrong because of wrong information only. It's like a good computer; if it is given wrong information it will come up with the wrong result, it has to.

KRISHNAMURTI: Yes, that's right, that's a good simile. You see that organized religions have no truth in them. You see it totally and you do not go back and organize religious ideas – it is finished for you. And your action will be totally logical, never contradictory.

DAVID BOHM: Yes. But there is a feeling that human beings are not capable of this kind of perfection, you see.

KRISHNAMURTI: It's not perfection, sir. I don't see it as perfection. I see it as a man who is aware, sensitive, attentive and sees the danger, and therefore doesn't touch it.

DAVID BOHM: I have talked with a few of the scientists, especially with one of them, and I think he has some idea of what you mean. But he is rather dubious that a human being could really be that sensitive, that ready to drop all his attachments.

KRISHNAMURTI: I don't see why it should be inhuman, if one can put it that way. Why should it be inhuman to see truth?

DAVID BOHM: I think you are right. There is no reason, it's merely our tradition.

KRISHNAMURTI: That's it, that thickness of the wall which thought has created.

DAVID BOHM: People have made the tradition of being modest, of saying 'It is only human to err', and so on.

KRISHNAMURTI: There is no question of modesty about this. I think one has to have a great sense of humility to see truth. The expression of it is not done with humility, it has nothing to do with 'me'.

DAVID BOHM: Yes, I understand that.

KRISHNAMURTI: Let's go back to our question.

Is there a space in consciousness which is not created by thought? Is there any part of consciousness, a little corner, which thought has not touched?

DAVID BOHM: I should think it's impossible, because thought is one structure; every part of thought touches every other part, in my view.

KRISHNAMURTI: I see that. Every thought touches the various other parts.

DAVID BOHM: Either directly or indirectly, they all touch.

KRISHNAMURTI: Quite. All fragments within consciousness are related. So there is no space, no hidden spot where thought has not touched. As we said, all thoughts, all fragments are related to each other. That being so, then what brings about the act of perception?

DAVID BOHM: You frequently ask this sort of question to which the answer is not clear.

KRISHNAMURTI: I think the answer is clear, sir, when we say thought comes to an end.

DAVID BOHM: That's what we said before, yes. But then you ask, what brings it to an end?

KRISHNAMURTI: My first question is: does thought see its own movement, and therefore thought itself sees the futility of it and stops?

DAVID BOHM: It doesn't seem to me that thought has that power, because thought deals with fragments. All that thought perceives, it perceives in fragments. It might see the futility in a fragmentary way.

KRISHNAMURTI: Yes, and therefore it can contradict itself.

DAVID BOHM: One part will try to stop and the other part keeps on going.

KRISHNAMURTI: So you are saying, thought cannot see itself as a whole. Only a mind that sees the whole sees truth, and to see the whole, thought has to come to an end. Now how does this happen? Not 'how' in the sense of a method, a system, but what brings this about? If you say it is attention, it's not quite that.

DAVID BOHM: Why do you say it's not attention?

KRISHNAMURTI: Because when you are not attentive you see things which you've never seen before.

DAVID BOHM: Let's get this clear. You are saying there is a perception beyond attention, which comes unexpectedly.

KRISHNAMURTI: It cannot be invited. It's like saying, 'I'll be attentive in order to receive truth.' That's nonsense.

DAVID BOHM: The word 'attention' means basically to stretch yourself towards something. Now, you are saying that, in some sense, when you are not stretched out, something may come unexpectedly.

KRISHNAMURTI: That's why when you say it is attention, I say it's not quite that.

DAVID BOHM: But is attention still connected with thought?

KRISHNAMURTI: No, concentration is connected with thought.

DAVID BOHM: But there is an attention, you say, which is not connected with thought, but still it's not what we want.

KRISHNAMURTI: No, it's not the whole.

DAVID BOHM: Not quite what we need.

KRISHNAMURTI: So there is an awareness which is not concentration, an awareness in which there is no choice, an awareness which moves – and attention. In that attention there is a stretching out to capture. That is attention in the field of reality to capture something. To me that's not sufficient.

DAVID BOHM: Would you say attention means stretching out from awareness?

KRISHNAMURTI: Yes.

DAVID BOHM: Then it's not sufficient.

KRISHNAMURTI: Not sufficient, if we understand the meaning of that word to be 'to stretch out'.

DAVID BOHM: Yes, but suppose I said that I am aware of something and I stretch to it, I want to capture it. The very word 'perceive' means to capture. And that is not thought, but it's still based on memory.

KRISHNAMURTI: It's not quite enough.

DAVID BOHM: It's beyond memory but it's not quite enough, because you say thought is the movement of memory.

KRISHNAMURTI: So there must be a sense of non-being, there must be a sense of nothingness. When there is choice in awareness, then it is not.

DAVID BOHM: Yes, but we were talking about awareness without choice, then we go beyond attention.

KRISHNAMURTI: And we say, attention is still not enough.

DAVID BOHM: What is attention? Is it a kind of energy?

KRISHNAMURTI: Attention is summation of energy, but that's not quite enough.

DAVID BOHM: It's the summation of the human energy.

KRISHNAMURTI: It's a human energy, that is not enough. Obviously. So if the mind, going through all this, comes to absolute nothingness – nothingness being not a thing in it – that is more than summation of energy; it is far beyond!

DAVID BOHM: Attention is summation of the energy of the human being, and you are saying there may be an energy beyond that.

KRISHNAMURTI: That's right.

DAVID BOHM: Which it would be wrong to call cosmic, but still it's something beyond what we would call the power of the individual.

KRISHNAMURTI: Beyond the human energy. There is a danger in this, because one can imagine that the mind has seen all that.

DAVID BOHM: You have gone through discovering all this. In other words, what you are saying now is a discovery. Or were you seeing it this way all your life?

KRISHNAMURTI: I'm afraid so.

DAVID BOHM: Then it brings up another question, which we have discussed once before, that for some odd reason you were that way and the rest of us were not. I mean, some combination of tendencies and environment makes a person conditioned.

KRISHNAMURTI: Yes, but he had been through all that. A human being going through all that gets conditioned. Another human being going through that is not conditioned.

DAVID BOHM: It's not clear what the difference is. Why is there a difference?

KRISHNAMURTI: There are two human beings, one gets conditioned and the other doesn't. How has it happened that one did not get conditioned? Is it a lack of good health at the beginning, that he was very ill, diseased, and therefore he never listened to anything? Did conditioning never penetrate because the body wasn't healthy and therefore he didn't receive anything?

DAVID BOHM: I see, and then by the time he could receive, he was stronger.

KRISHNAMURTI: Yes, therefore he never entered it.

DAVID BOHM: It never took hold.

KRISHNAMURTI: The other took hold.

DAVID BOHM: In the course of development, children go through stages of tremendous openness to something and at a certain stage that development is no longer possible.

KRISHNAMURTI: The other human being, the one who is not conditioned, is open.

DAVID BOHM: Yes, he remains open.

KRISHNAMURTI: Now how does this happen? There are several theories about this. One is that the entity who is not conditioned has had many previous lives.

DAVID BOHM: Yes, I am aware of that theory.

KRISHNAMURTI: And the other theory is – I won't use the Asian language, I want to avoid it – that there is a reservoir of goodness.
Is there goodness in the world? And is there evil in the world?

DAVID BOHM: That is a point we could discuss, because it's not clear.

KRISHNAMURTI: I mean there are these two, the evil and the good. I'm just saying, there is this theory. I wouldn't call them 'principles', that would be an idea.

DAVID BOHM: You sound as if you are calling it a substance. They almost seem like substances, or energies.

DR PARCHURE: Two forces.

KRISHNAMURTI: Let's keep to that word 'forces'. There are these two forces, and some Asians believe that the good is with those who have advanced spiritually, that they hold it. And evil is held by those people who are battling with the good. This idea exists throughout the ages; the Egyptians believed it, the Romans, the Persians and so on. It sounds ridiculous, I'm just offering it for inspection and destruction. That goodness can penetrate into a human being and so keep him whole.

DAVID BOHM: Yes, to resist the conditioning.

KRISHNAMURTI: To keep him whole, not 'resist'.

DAVID BOHM: No, not resist, but he becomes impervious to the conditioning.

KRISHNAMURTI: Yes, impervious, nothing penetrates. The point is that the force of goodness is holding a certain human being who has very little selfishness, who has very little self.

DAVID BOHM: Yes, but that begs the question, you see.

KRISHNAMURTI: Of course, I'm just giving you the idea. Another theory is that from childhood he was ill, not capable of receiving, mentally retarded, vague.

DAVID BOHM: The other theory is that the unconditioned person at the beginning was not healthy enough to pay much attention to the world and then, by the time he could pay attention, he was free of it. That may be a reasonable theory.

KRISHNAMURTI: Yes, that seems fairly reasonable. But that doesn't give you the whole of it. I'm not saying I'm unconditioned; it would be silly on my part to say it.

So the problem then is, how does this perception which is beyond attention, beyond awareness, beyond concentration, come about? Must every child become ill, be unhealthy?

DAVID BOHM: Most children who are unhealthy just succumb to even worse things. It's surely very fortuitous that it would produce this effect.

KRISHNAMURTI: Can this be cultivated? Obviously not. Cultivation implies time, and all the rest of it. So what brings this about? Shall we go into it a little?

There must be awareness. Awareness means being sensitive, sensitive not to one's own desire, which is very easy, but sensitive to the environment, to other people. And in that awareness any choice is still the movement of thought. So, in awareness the movement of thought as choice comes to an end.

DAVID BOHM: Yes. Would you say that choice is the essence of the movement of thought?

KRISHNAMURTI: Yes.

DAVID BOHM: In other words, that's the real root of it.

KRISHNAMURTI: Yes, I think that's logical, too. From that attention there is affection, care and a sense of deep communication. You say something and the mind receives it at its depth – not superficially. And that is not enough, obviously.

DAVID BOHM: This is all still the ordinary human individual getting into his depth.

KRISHNAMURTI: Yes.

DAVID BOHM: Thought, we could say, is rather superficial, it's merely a very small part of the operation of the brain and the nerves. In awareness and attention we go much deeper.

KRISHNAMURTI: Yes, quite right. So love in attention is different from the love which exists in the field of reality.

DAVID BOHM: In the field of reality it's not love.

KRISHNAMURTI: That's right. So in attention there is this quality of love. I love you, therefore I receive you profoundly, therefore communication is not verbal. And *that* is not enough.

DAVID BOHM: It's still a depth of the human individual.

KRISHNAMURTI: Yes. Therefore the next question is: can this consciousness be completely empty of its content? Which means, there is nothing inside it, nothing created by thought, by circumstances, by temperament, by imagination, by tendency, by capacity.

DAVID BOHM: When you are aware of the environment, that's not what you mean by 'nothing inside'. In other words, that includes still an awareness of the environment.

KRISHNAMURTI: Of course. Here there is nothing. Is that possible? Is one imagining it?

DAVID BOHM: Well, yes.

KRISHNAMURTI: We are not imagining it, because we have seen right from the beginning that thought is contradictory. Part of that thought is desire which is contradictory. So thought, desire, in their movement must create contradiction and fragmentation. And we move from there to the sense of one fragment controlling, opposing, resisting other fragments of thought. That is concentration. We see that. Then there is awareness in which thought enters as choice, and *that* is seen. Then there is this attention in which there is affection, which didn't exist in awareness or in concentration.

DAVID BOHM: Did you say it exists in attention but not in awareness?

KRISHNAMURTI: Yes, attention has this quality of love. Then you ask: what do you mean by it, how do you know? And that is *still* not enough. So the next question is: can this consciousness be totally empty and therefore it is not consciousness as we know it?

DAVID BOHM: Will it still be consciousness, then?

KRISHNAMURTI: That's it.

DAVID BOHM: Well, would it?

KRISHNAMURTI: No, it wouldn't. I say that consciousness as we know it is its content, it is the movement – wide or narrow – of thought. In nothingness there is no movement at all. But it has its own movement as energy – whatever it is – which then can operate in the field of reality.

DAVID BOHM: We have to clarify what you say, because you say 'it has no movement', yet you say 'it has movement'.

KRISHNAMURTI: The movement which we know is time – from here to there, and all the rest of it. Can we use 'emptiness', in the sense that a cup is empty?

DAVID BOHM: That means it has the possibility to take content. You may not use it in that sense.

KRISHNAMURTI: No, I'm not using it in that sense.

DAVID BOHM: If you say the cup is empty, it implies that something is going to fill it up.

KRISHNAMURTI: Quite. No, it's not that. There is nothingness, but it has a movement which is not the movement of thought, which is not the movement of time.

DAVID BOHM: So now we have two kinds of movement, there is time and something else.

KRISHNAMURTI: Yes.

DAVID BOHM: It occurs to me also that time is contradiction. Could we say that when thought reaches a contradiction it jumps to another thought, and to another one, and that jump is time?

KRISHNAMURTI: Right. It still moves.

DAVID BOHM: Therefore the movement of thought, the very essence of psychological time, is contradiction.

KRISHNAMURTI: Sir, we are asking if there is an energy which is not contradictory, which is not jumping from one pattern to another pattern, a movement which is totally unrelated to the time-movement?

DAVID BOHM: One way of looking at it is that there is that energy which reveals itself in the order of reality in time. Does that make sense?

KRISHNAMURTI: Yes.

DAVID BOHM: It manifests, it reveals itself. Right?

KRISHNAMURTI: Yes, that's right. Can you repeat it once more?

DAVID BOHM: A view that I've heard is that there is a movement you talk about, the timeless. It does not exist in time but it manifests in time, or reveals itself in time.

KRISHNAMURTI: Which is what we are saying in a different way, aren't we?

DAVID BOHM: Yes. Several different people have said that, the ancients and also some of the Indians in America.

KRISHNAMURTI: Yes, and the Asians; in India, too, they say that it manifests itself in the field of reality.

DAVID BOHM: And time, yes. Is that acceptable to you?

KRISHNAMURTI: I don't quite see it that way yet. I am beginning to look at it. Are we putting it in different words, that the human being who perceives truth can function in the field of reality, and therefore his perception is never distorted, even though he functions?

DAVID BOHM: Yes, but other people, watching him, will see him functioning in the field of reality, in which case we could call it a manifestation.

KRISHNAMURTI: Yes, a manifestation, the Avatar – a Sanskrit word. Would that be true? That is, you as a human being perceive truth. You have that perception and you operate in the field of reality. You manifest that truth in the field of reality. Therefore that manifestation must be the essence of intelligence which cannot be distorted.

May I put a question this way? Why should truth operate in the field of reality?

DAVID BOHM: Well, that's the point that has probably been worrying me in the back of my mind.

KRISHNAMURTI: I caught you! Why should it operate in the field of reality?

DAVID BOHM: Well, let's just say that people generally accept that it does. Perhaps it doesn't.

KRISHNAMURTI: That's what I'm asking. Why should it operate? Why should we take it for granted that it operates?

DAVID BOHM: I can see why we take it for granted, it doesn't mean that it's right.

KRISHNAMURTI: No, I don't think it is right.

DAVID BOHM: We take it for granted because we hope that we will have something in the field of reality to keep us right.

KRISHNAMURTI: To have a string of hope. We have accepted as a part of tradition, as a part of our conditioning, our hope, desire and thought, that the human being who perceives truth can and does operate in the field of reality. You and I come and say, why should he?

DAVID BOHM: Perhaps he shouldn't.

KRISHNAMURTI: I think this may be the actuality rather than the desire which creates the actuality.

DAVID BOHM: Perhaps you would like to change it and say, the man operates in actuality. You would have to accept that, wouldn't you?

KRISHNAMURTI: Of course.

DAVID BOHM: But perhaps you say the field of reality is twisted and delusory, anyway; it's never quite right.

KRISHNAMURTI: That is a very dangerous thing. Sir, if truth operates in reality, then there is the assumption that man contains truth, that consciousness contains truth.

DAVID BOHM: Well, at least it has a link to truth.

KRISHNAMURTI: That is the same thing put differently: 'In man there is the highest principle.'

DAVID BOHM: I think the most subtle way is to say that in man the highest principle operates, though it may be beyond him.

KRISHNAMURTI: I question that.

We are asking, why should truth enter into the field of reality at all? Why should the highest principle manifest itself in the field of reality? You can put it ten different ways – why should it? We *want* it to operate, because it is a part of our desire, part of our thinking.

DAVID BOHM: We would like to feel that it can operate to bring order into reality.

KRISHNAMURTI: Yes, so we cling to that idea. And if I don't cling to that idea, the next question is: how do I, living in the world of reality, bring order to it?

DAVID BOHM: Yes, but then are you living in the world of reality?

KRISHNAMURTI: Suppose a human being is living in reality, and he says, 'I see this terrible mess, how do I bring order into it?'

DAVID BOHM: It almost follows from what you say that it cannot be done.

KRISHNAMURTI: That's just it. Because thought cannot bring order into the world of reality in which human beings live.

DAVID BOHM: No, thought itself is disorder.

KRISHNAMURTI: So people say, 'Leave that alone, get away from it, join a monastery, go away by yourself, form a community of equals, because you can't bring order into this disorder.'

DAVID BOHM: It seems to me the right approach is to consider the actuality. You see, as we said at the very beginning, this reality may be real, but it's false. Therefore truth cannot operate in the false.

KRISHNAMURTI: Yes, truth cannot operate in the false. But I am surrounded by it, I *am* false. You follow, sir? I *am* false, because what thought has created psychologically *is* false. And how can truth operate in the false?

DAVID BOHM: It doesn't.

KRISHNAMURTI: Obviously it cannot. But can there be order in the field of the false? Because that is what we need.

DAVID BOHM: Yes, we can have some relative order.

KRISHNAMURTI: So you are saying order is relative.

DAVID BOHM: I mean we cannot fix it.

KRISHNAMURTI: Order is relative, and also there is an order of truth which is supreme order.

DAVID BOHM: Yes, but that couldn't be in the field of reality, from what you are saying. I mean, we could bring relative order into our lives in the field of reality.

KRISHNAMURTI: But that isn't good enough. That is what the politicians are doing. Therefore human beings introduce an element of divine order, of truth and hope, and they pray to receive the grace of that divine order which will put more than relative order into their lives. That is not good enough. It is illogical, even verbally it is totally unacceptable.

So these are the two problems. I want order here in the world of reality, because order means security, safety, protection. I must have that for everybody, and thought cannot produce that order, because thought itself has created the disorder, thought itself is fragmentary. So thought cannot bring the order which is essential for human beings. Human beings can invent God, or a source of energy which is truth, which will help man to bring about order. Thought can project a truth – but that's out, I don't accept that.

Yet I need order. Not relative order, we've played that game for centuries. I need absolute order here. Why can't I have absolute order here without invoking or looking to truth?

DAVID BOHM: Let's go into that. At first sight you could say that what determines the reality is thought, and thought is contradictory. What is going to make thought non-contradictory?

KRISHNAMURTI: So I introduce something which I hope will bring order.

DAVID BOHM: Non-contradiction.

KRISHNAMURTI: And that is the invention of thought, too.

DAVID BOHM: Yes, but I don't see how you can bring about what you would want to have.

KRISHNAMURTI: But intelligent, healthy, normal human beings have the necessity for complete order here.

DAVID BOHM: Let's try to look at that, because you see that the whole world is in almost complete disorder and we see no obvious way of bringing order. People have tried in countless ways and as long as the world is ruled by thought, the disorder will continue.

KRISHNAMURTI: That's it. I accept that, because you have shown it to me logically. I say that's good enough, I don't want anything more. I will see, control, and shape thought.

DAVID BOHM: But can you?

KRISHNAMURTI: Thought itself says, 'I will be orderly'. I know I'm disorderly, I jump from pattern to pattern, there is contradiction, and so on. I know all this, but I will be very watchful. And that very self-recollected watchfulness will have order, without introducing an outside agency which will bring order.

DAVID BOHM: Is it your view that that can be done?

KRISHNAMURTI: I am asking that following the question: why should truth operate in the field of reality?

DR PARCHURE: Do you get awareness as a product of thought?

KRISHNAMURTI: No, thought says, 'I have created this awful mess and I can't do anything about it.' Therefore thought abstains from the movement to which it is accustomed, and says, 'I see this, I won't operate in that way, I will abstain, I will hold, I will be intelligent.'

Can that take place?

DAVID BOHM: We have to look into that, because we have to ask: what is there in thought that will allow this to take place? Is thought in some way non-mechanical?

DR PARCHURE: I feel that thought has in it some element which is not necessarily completely mechanical.

KRISHNAMURTI: You are saying thought is not mechanical?

DR PARCHURE: There is some part which is not quite mechanical; it can produce some order in itself without appealing to truth.

KRISHNAMURTI: So parts of thought are healthy, parts of it are unhealthy? And we say, no, there is no healthy thought.

DR PARCHURE: I am using 'reality' as synonymous with 'thought', because you are using it that way.

KRISHNAMURTI: We are using it that way, bearing it in mind.

DR PARCHURE: In the field of reality there are sufferings which demand orderliness.

KRISHNAMURTI: In the field of reality, you are saying, suffering itself says, 'No more'. Wait, let's look at it. That feeling of intense suffering brought about by thought says, 'No more'. But the 'no more' is the action of thought.

DR PARCHURE: Maybe, yes.

KRISHNAMURTI: Not maybe.

DR PARCHURE: Yes, it is.

KRISHNAMURTI: So it is still in the field of contradiction.

DR PARCHURE: But there is a little order in it.

KRISHNAMURTI: We have been through that. I don't want to live in a *little* order.

DR PARCHURE: Then you cannot talk of total order in the field of reality.

KRISHNAMURTI: You are saying the same thing. In the field of reality there can only be relative order. We said that right from the beginning. I am not satisfied with that; I don't want relative order, I want order because I see the poor man who will never know what it is to sleep in a good, healthy bed, with clean sheets. He has never had proper food, and I, as a human being, see that, and I say, 'This is terrible, there must be *order!*' Not relative order. We are fed, *and he is not fed.*

DAVID BOHM: We could have some improvement; maybe we could have everybody fed.

KRISHNAMURTI: I arrange it in the field of reality that everybody is fed. In that situation, don't let there be tyranny feeding me, don't you become the tyrant; that will create disorder. So if human beings can be fed without creating tyranny, that is order.

DAVID BOHM: That is only a hope.

KRISHNAMURTI: That's it.

DAVID BOHM: I think that it has been achieved at times to have everybody fed, but it would not be possible without some authority.

KRISHNAMURTI: The Incas had a marvellous system – but there was authority. And there was the authority of the Pharaohs. I don't want that kind of order. My ordinary human intelligence says, we've been through all that, I don't want it. Therefore you introduce an order brought about by truth. I say truth cannot enter into the world of reality. We demand it to enter, but it may not enter. I'm stuck with this. You say truth can enter into the field of reality and operate there, and another human says that truth is something so absolute it cannot be relative, it cannot be made by thought to be a relative operation in the field of reality. Then you say to me, 'I'm not interested in truth if it cannot operate and bring order here; what's the point of it?' Then it's a wild dream, just a pleasurable fantasy.

DR PARCHURE: We have said that there is only one relation possible.

KRISHNAMURTI: We have said that truth may have a relationship to reality, but reality has no relationship to truth.

DAVID BOHM: But now we deny the point of the investigation.

KRISHNAMURTI: Yes, we are saying it may have no relationship.

DAVID BOHM: I think we could say this: the spirit, the investigation, is what we were talking about, the dialectic. We do something and we explore it, and it may reveal contradiction and we must drop it. So that is the approach.

KRISHNAMURTI: Absolutely.

DR PARCHURE: Do you say that in the field of reality there are not sufficient springs to bring order into this field?

KRISHNAMURTI: I don't know. Maybe. Maybe in the field of reality thought itself sees it cannot act any more.

DAVID BOHM: Yes, I understand what you say. Now that would imply that thought has the possibility of being not entirely mechanical.

KRISHNAMURTI: I don't accept that.

DAVID BOHM: But can the mechanism see it?

KRISHNAMURTI: Thought is mechanical, you can't go beyond that.

DAVID BOHM: Now, is the mechanism going to see this?

KRISHNAMURTI: Can thought see that it is making a mistake?

DAVID BOHM: Obviously, but with the help of awareness and attention and so on. Thought can see it has made a mistake, but it seems it has to have the help of those elements.

KRISHNAMURTI: Quite. So what has a human being left? He says, 'I live in a world of disorder and I must have complete order there, not a little order. The only healthy way to live is in complete order.' And as I do not have complete order, I then move from there to controlling thought. And thought then says, 'There must be something beyond.' That 'beyond' is a contradiction to this, because it is the projection of thought. Therefore it is still within the realm of reality, within the realm of thought.

DAVID BOHM: Yes. Now, can we find a solution to this in the realm of reality? That is what you're asking.

KRISHNAMURTI: Yes.

DAVID BOHM: And therefore we may have to deny some of the things that we have just been saying, if necessary.

KRISHNAMURTI: I don't think it can!

DAVID BOHM: It can't. So there is no solution in the field of reality.

KRISHNAMURTI: There is no solution in the field of reality to have absolute order. And human beings need absolute order.

DAVID BOHM: That's right. But can thought abstain, or suspend itself to the point where it does not create disorder?

KRISHNAMURTI: Just a minute, sir. I see my life is in disorder; I am conscious of it, and I realize that disorder has been created by thought. So thought cannot bring about order. That is a fact, that is an actuality, that is so.

DAVID BOHM: If thought assumes that it is the only energy, then it says, 'I must operate.' If it says that, it covers everything. But if thought says, 'I abstain from operating...'

KRISHNAMURTI: No. Must it say that, or does something else take place?

DAVID BOHM: What is it?

KRISHNAMURTI: I live in disorder. I see disorder, contradiction, and I also see the fact that thought brings about this disorder. I see the danger of it. When there is the perception of real danger, thought doesn't act, it is a shock to thought. Just as beauty is a shock to thought, danger is a shock to thought. So thought holds. And in that holding of thought is order.

Let's put it this way. We go to Gstaad and we see all those marvellous mountains, and your thought is blown away. Just the beauty of it drives away all movement of thought. And it is the same when thought sees tremendous danger.

DAVID BOHM: That's with the aid of attention and awareness, and so on. But thought sees it.

KRISHNAMURTI: When a car is rushing towards me, thought sees it and jumps out of the way. The jumping away from danger is order.

DAVID BOHM: Yes, but the perception of the danger may not be maintained.

KRISHNAMURTI: Or one may not see the danger at all. One does not see the danger of nationalism, which means most of us are neurotic. When you have had ten wars, and still keep on repeating them, that is a neurotic movement.

DAVID BOHM: Yes, that's part of the problem – that thought dulls perception and prevents it from operating.

KRISHNAMURTI: Or is it because I am conditioned?

DAVID BOHM: I am conditioned to do just that.

KRISHNAMURTI: Now you come along and educate me to be unconditioned, to see the danger of all this. And as you educate me, I see the danger, I won't do it.

So why should truth enter into the field of reality?

DAVID BOHM: What does truth do then? I mean, what is its action?

KRISHNAMURTI: What is its function, what does it do, what is its value? Not in the sense of merchandise, or usage, but is it employable? What is its quality, what is its nature?

You see, we say, 'Truth is supreme intelligence' – and we are caught. We are asking: can that intelligence operate in the field of reality? If it does, then it can bring about absolute order. But that truth is not to be achieved, or gained, or perceived through education, through culture, through the medium of thought.

DAVID BOHM: No. When you say truth does not operate in the field of reality, again it becomes unclear, ambiguous.

KRISHNAMURTI: Truth cannot enter into the field of reality.

DAVID BOHM: What is their relation?

KRISHNAMURTI: Sir, what has goodness to do with evil?

DAVID BOHM: Well, nothing.

KRISHNAMURTI: Why should we want goodness to operate on evil? Cover it, change it, modify it?

DAVID BOHM: Yes, but would it be right to say that goodness may dissolve evil? It may end even that.

KRISHNAMURTI: Has goodness a relationship with evil? If it has, then it can do something. If it has no relationship with evil, it can't do anything.

DAVID BOHM: Then you ask the question: when will evil come to an end?

KRISHNAMURTI: When will evil come to an end? Evil being created by man?

DAVID BOHM: Yes, by his thought.

KRISHNAMURTI: By his thought. Then you come back to the same question. It will end when thought comes to an end.

DR PARCHURE: Has goodness any power over thought?

KRISHNAMURTI: Goodness has no relationship with thought, goodness has no relationship with evil. If it has a relationship, it is an opposite, and all opposites contain each other. So that's out. So goodness has no relationship to evil. And Dr Bohm asks if evil will go on. Because it has no relationship, of course it will. Can human beings see the evil of thought, the contradiction of thought?

So our concern is to show man that thought can never solve its problems, not to ask 'What will?'

DAVID BOHM: Could you put it like this – while thought is going on?

KRISHNAMURTI: Yes. While there is the movement of thought as time and so on, evil and misery will go on. That is a tremendous revelation to me, when you state that. Because to me thought has been tremendously important. I function in that.

DAVID BOHM: Yes, it's very revolutionary; and I ask, 'What will I do without thought?'

KRISHNAMURTI: Exactly. It is a tremendous revelation. *And I stop there.*

I don't know what is going to happen. That is the beauty of this. I listen and it is revealed, and there is no action. I just watch. *I live in that revelation.*

DAVID BOHM: And that is the movement which is beyond attention.

KRISHNAMURTI: A little bit beyond attention. I have paid attention to him; I have listened to him; he has shown me, he has pointed out; I am full of this extraordinary statement. I don't know how it will operate, I don't know how I will live. That is enough. I have seen this thing. And *it* will operate. *I* am not going to take action. *It* will do something, I don't have to do anything. Before, I was accustomed to doing something; now he says, 'Don't.'

To hurt another is evil. I am taking that as an example. We went into all that. We know what it means. In the deepest sense of that word, to deeply hurt somebody psychologically is evil. He tells me that, and I receive it without any resistance – resistance is thought. It has entered into my womb, into my mind, into my whole being. And it operates, it functions, it moves. Truth has its own vitality, its own movement.

It's a wrong question for me to ask what place truth has in reality.

Brockwood Park, 22 June 1975

4 Thought and perception

KRISHNAMURTI: Why has mankind given such tremendous importance to thought?

DAVID BOHM: You have pointed out that thought gives security in many senses, not only in the sense of psychological security, but also material security.

KRISHNAMURTI: Yes, thought in itself is not secure.

DAVID BOHM: Thought cannot be secure, it's a mere reflection.

KRISHNAMURTI: Yes, therefore it cannot be secure in itself and seeks security outside.

DAVID BOHM: But why does it seek security?

KRISHNAMURTI: Because thought is constantly changing, constantly moving.

DAVID BOHM: But that doesn't explain why it's not satisfied to just be that.

KRISHNAMURTI: Because it sees its own perishable nature.

DAVID BOHM: Why should it want to be imperishable?

KRISHNAMURTI: Because that which is imperishable is its security.

DAVID BOHM: If thought were content to say, 'I'm insecure, I'm impermanent', then it would be like nature, it would just say, 'I'm here today and tomorrow I'm different.'

KRISHNAMURTI: Of course. But I am not satisfied with that. Is it because of attachment?

DAVID BOHM: But what *is* attachment? Why should thought attach itself to anything? Why shouldn't it say, 'I'm just thought, I'm just a reflection'?

KRISHNAMURTI: But you're giving to thought considerable intelligence. If it says, 'I'm just like nature, I just come and go in constant movement...'

DAVID BOHM: Now are you saying that thought is mechanical, that's why it's doing this. Then we have to see why a mechanism should necessarily seek security. A machine doesn't seek anything in particular; we can set up a machine and it just goes.

KRISHNAMURTI: Of course. As long as there is energy, it'll go on working.

DAVID BOHM: If it breaks down, that's the end of it.

KRISHNAMURTI: But does thought realize that it is mechanical?

DAVID BOHM: No, but thought made a mistake, there is something incorrect in its content; which is, thought does not know it's mechanical. But does that mean that thought thinks it is not mechanical?

KRISHNAMURTI: Sir, a mechanical thing doesn't get hurt.

DAVID BOHM: No, it just functions.

KRISHNAMURTI: Whereas thought gets hurt.

DAVID BOHM: And thought has pleasure.

KRISHNAMURTI: Yes, pleasure, pain, and all the rest of it. Let's stick to one thing. It gets hurt. Why does it get hurt? Because of the image and so on. It has created the image, and in the thing that it has created it is seeking security, isn't it?

DAVID BOHM: Yes, it is not clear why it ever began to seek that kind of security. If it began as a mechanism, there was no...

KRISHNAMURTI: This is rather interesting, isn't it? Why does thought not realize it is mechanical? Why does it suppose that it is something different from a machine?

DAVID BOHM: Yes, it may in some sense suppose it has intelligence and feeling and that it's a living thing, rather than mechanical.

KRISHNAMURTI: I think that's the root of it, isn't it? It thinks it's living. And therefore it attributes to itself the quality of non-mechanical existence. Thought is clever, giving itself qualities which basically it does not have. Why does it do it?

DAVID BOHM: You were saying that thought somehow can realize it is mechanical, which would imply that it had some intelligence.

KRISHNAMURTI: Yes. Does thought realize that it is mechanical or is it perception that sees it?

DAVID BOHM: That would seem to be a change from what you said the other day.

KRISHNAMURTI: I'm just investigating.

DAVID BOHM: It's made of parts which are put together and so on. Now, if there is a perception that thought is mechanical, then the intelligence is in the perception.

KRISHNAMURTI: Are we saying, sir, that thought has in itself the quality of intelligence, of perception, and therefore it perceives itself as being mechanical?

DAVID BOHM: That would seem strange.

KRISHNAMURTI: Or there is perception, and that perception says thought is mechanical.

DAVID BOHM: Yes, we call that truth.

KRISHNAMURTI: Yes, but there are two things. Either the thought in itself has this sense of perception, this sense of intelligence, and therefore realizes that it's mechanical, or there is perception which is truth, and that perception says thought is mechanical.

DAVID BOHM: Yes, but the first idea seems to be a contradiction.

KRISHNAMURTI: Yes. Does this answer why thought is fragmentary?

DAVID BOHM: If thought is mechanical, then it will have to be fragmentary.

KRISHNAMURTI: Can't thought realize it's mechanical?

DAVID BOHM: Previously you were saying there would be a conscious awareness of the nature of thought and thought would then come to order.

KRISHNAMURTI: We must go back to something else, then. The things that consciousness contains are put together by thought. All the content of that consciousness is the product of thought; consciousness *is* thought.

DAVID BOHM: Yes, it's the whole process.

KRISHNAMURTI: Yes. Does thought see all this, or is there pure perception without thought which then says thought is mechanical?

DAVID BOHM: Then how does thought know what to do? We were saying the other day that when there is perception of truth...

KRISHNAMURTI: Action takes place.

DAVID BOHM: ...action takes place, and thought becomes aware of that action.

KRISHNAMURTI: Yes, that's right.

DAVID BOHM: Now, in becoming aware of that action, is thought mechanical?

KRISHNAMURTI: No, thought then is not mechanical.

DAVID BOHM: You have to say that thought changes its nature. That's the point we have to get hold of, that thought does not have a fixed nature. Is that the point?

KRISHNAMURTI: Yes, sir.

DAVID BOHM: I think that much of the discussion tends to imply that thought has a fixed nature, but now we say thought can change.

KRISHNAMURTI: Yes, thought *does* change.

DAVID BOHM: Yes, but I mean it can change fundamentally.

KRISHNAMURTI: Wait, I'm beginning to see something – we're both beginning to see something. We say total perception is truth. That perception operates in actuality. There is perception which is truth, and that can only act in actuality. Look, sir, put it round the other way. I perceive something totally, which is not the act of thought.

DAVID BOHM: Yes, that is a direct act.

KRISHNAMURTI: Yes, that is direct perception. That perception acts directly.

DAVID BOHM: Without thought.

KRISHNAMURTI: That's what I want to find out.

DAVID BOHM: Yes. When there is perception of danger, it acts immediately, without thought.

KRISHNAMURTI: That's right. Thought then can become aware of the act, and translate it into words. That is, there is a total perception, which is truth. That perception acts in the field of reality. That action is not the product of thought, but because it is an action of the whole, thought has undergone a change.

DAVID BOHM: You say thought is part of the whole, thought is contained within the whole and therefore it is changed. Is that what you're saying?

KRISHNAMURTI: No, I'm just investigating. When it sees the whole, that's the truth.

DAVID BOHM: The whole is different, because of the perception.

KRISHNAMURTI: It is not fragmented.

DAVID BOHM: No, it's one whole, but different.

KRISHNAMURTI: Yes, and it acts. The action is not the product of thought, it is not put together by thought. That's clear. Then what is the relationship of thought to that act?

DAVID BOHM: We could say that thought is a material process, based on the brain cells. Now the action of perception will somehow act on the brain cells, won't it?

KRISHNAMURTI: That's the point; it does. Quite right, sir.

DAVID BOHM: And therefore thought must be different.

KRISHNAMURTI: Quite right. That is, sir, you see something totally and that total perception is different from the fragmentary perception, which has been the nature of the activity of the brain. When there is this total perception and action, it must affect the brain cells.

DAVID BOHM: Suppose, in affecting the brain cells, it may change the nature of thought.

KRISHNAMURTI: Wait, it's rather tenuous. It is a shock, it's something totally new to the brain.

DAVID BOHM: And therefore perception totally penetrates the physical structure of the brain.

KRISHNAMURTI: Yes. Let's be simple about it. If you see that division, fragmentation is a tremendous danger – if you really see it – doesn't it affect your whole way of thinking?

DAVID BOHM: Yes, and thought has developed a way of preventing this effect from taking place.

KRISHNAMURTI: That's it, that's what I want to get at. Thought resists it.

DAVID BOHM: But why? A machine would not resist.

KRISHNAMURTI: No, because it is a habit. It is conditioned to that, it remains in that groove. And perception comes along and shakes that.

DAVID BOHM: Yes, but thought stabilizes itself, it holds to a fixed position. If we look at it this way, thought hasn't got a fixed nature, it may be mechanical or it may be intelligent.

KRISHNAMURTI: No, I wouldn't give the word 'intelligence' to thought for the moment.

DAVID BOHM: Before, we said that thought may not have a fixed nature and needn't be mechanical.

KRISHNAMURTI: Thought functions in grooves, thought lives in habits, in memories, and a total perception does affect the whole structure.

DAVID BOHM: That's right, as a result of this perception thought is different.

KRISHNAMURTI: Yes, thought is different because of the perception.

DAVID BOHM: Because perception has penetrated the physical structure of the thought. But now we don't want to say it's intelligent. Let's say that thought would not cause trouble if it behaved like a machine, it would just function. Thought for some odd reason is trying to do more than behave like a machine.

KRISHNAMURTI: Yes, thought is trying to do more than a machine.

DAVID BOHM: Now, there is perception and awareness, and this may be recorded in thought. If perception affects the physical structure of the brain, this effect is somehow recorded in the content of memory.

KRISHNAMURTI: That's right. Just a minute, sir, I want to go back a little bit.

You perceive something totally. There is total perception of greed – let's take that for the moment. Because of that total perception, your activity is non-mechanical – the mechanical being the pursuing of greed by thought.

DAVID BOHM: But isn't there another part of thought which is mechanical but which is necessary? For example, the information contained in thought.

KRISHNAMURTI: Wait, I'm just coming to it. You perceive totally the nature and the structure of greed, and because you perceive, there is the ending of it. What place has thought then?

DAVID BOHM: It still has a mechanical function.

KRISHNAMURTI: No, it's finished – you're not greedy.

DAVID BOHM: Yes, but that also includes things that are other than greed, like the practical thought.

KRISHNAMURTI: But you're not greedy. That reaction, that momentum, that mechanical habit is over. Then what place has thought?

DAVID BOHM: But thought has *some* place if you want to find your way to go somewhere.

KRISHNAMURTI: What for? When I need a coat, I'll get it, but there is no greed.

DAVID BOHM: No, but thought is not identified with greed. You have thought which is rational. Greed is irrational thought.

KRISHNAMURTI: Yes, greed is irrational.

DAVID BOHM: But there is rational thought, for example, if you want to figure out something.

KRISHNAMURTI: When you perceive the totality of greed, something has happened to you.

DAVID BOHM: But are you saying there's no more thought?

KRISHNAMURTI: Thought is not necessary.

DAVID BOHM: Then how do you find your way? How do you use memory?

KRISHNAMURTI: Look, I'm no longer greedy, I've no need for thought in the field of perception and therefore thought doesn't enter into it at all.

DAVID BOHM: Not into perception, but it still has a place, apparently.

KRISHNAMURTI: I'm saying it has no place in greed. Where there is total perception, thought has no place.

DAVID BOHM: In that perception.

KRISHNAMURTI: Not only in the perception; thought doesn't exist any more with regard to that. You perceive that all belief is irrational, there is a perception of this total structure of belief, and then belief has no place in your thought, in your brain. If I perceive the total nature of belief, then it's over.

Then where does thought come into that which thought has created? I wonder if I'm conveying something. Look, sir, I perceive – for the moment I'm using 'I' – I perceive totally the nature of belief and fear, and all the rest of it. Because it is a total perception, belief as such doesn't exist in my thought, in my brain. Now, where does thought come into it?

DAVID BOHM: Not at that point.

KRISHNAMURTI: It's finished. Thought has no place when there is total perception. Thought operates only when there is a necessity for food, clothes or shelter. What do you say to that?

DAVID BOHM: Yes, that may be right.

KRISHNAMURTI: I want to question it, I want to go into it.

DAVID BOHM: But what we started with was to understand why thought has done what it has done. In other words, when there is total perception, then there is no place for thought. Now when we come to practical affairs, you could say we don't have total perception but we depend on information which has been accumulated and therefore we need thought.

KRISHNAMURTI: There, yes. I need it to build a house.

DAVID BOHM: And you depend on accumulated information, you cannot directly perceive how to build a house.

KRISHNAMURTI: Quite.

DAVID BOHM: But for psychological matters...

KRISHNAMURTI: When there is total perception, thought doesn't enter into the psychological process.

DAVID BOHM: Yes, it has no place in the psychological perception, although it may have a place in material perception.

KRISHNAMURTI: That's right.

DAVID BOHM: But still people will always ask why thought has gone wrong, why it has done all these strange things, why it has pushed itself to where it has no place.

KRISHNAMURTI: Could we say that thought creates illusion?

DAVID BOHM: Yes, but why should it, why does it want to? What makes it happen?

KRISHNAMURTI: Because thought has taken the place of perception.

DAVID BOHM: But why should it?

KRISHNAMURTI: Why should thought assume that it sees the whole?

DAVID BOHM: Or even that it sees *anything*.

KRISHNAMURTI: Does it happen, sir, that when there is total perception, that perception having no movement of thought, time, and so on, the mind uses thought only when necessary – and otherwise it's empty?

DAVID BOHM: I wonder if we could put it differently. Such a mind, when it uses thought, realizes that it *is* thought, it never supposes it's not thought.

KRISHNAMURTI: That's right. It realizes that it is thought and nothing else.

DAVID BOHM: If it is only thought, it has only a limited significance and we needn't consider it that important.

KRISHNAMURTI: That's right.

DAVID BOHM: I think the danger is that there is the mind which does not realize that this is thought. At some stage the mechanical process starts, which somehow does not acknowledge or does not know that it is mechanical.

KRISHNAMURTI: Yes. Would you also say that man never realized until recently that thought is physical and chemical, and therefore it assumed tremendous importance?

DAVID BOHM: Yes, it is certainly true that only recently has science shown the physical and chemical properties of thought.

KRISHNAMURTI: The habit, the conditioning, has been to say thought is the primary thing in life. Thought never realized it was limited. Is that what we are saying?

DAVID BOHM: That was part of it, yes.

KRISHNAMURTI: And we are also saying that, where there is total perception, a change in thought takes place.

DAVID BOHM: What happens to thought, then?

KRISHNAMURTI: Thought, being mechanical, can only operate mechanically, there is no psychological entity which thought can use.

DAVID BOHM: Let's clear this up a little. Let's say that there is a new invention, something new comes into thought, into the field of reality. But we say that might be a perception.

KRISHNAMURTI: I think it is, of course.

DAVID BOHM: Because of the perception, thought is different, but it remains mechanical.

KRISHNAMURTI: That's right, that's exactly what we are saying.

DAVID BOHM: It just changes the order of its operation through that perception and therefore the creativity is not in the thought itself but in the perception.

KRISHNAMURTI: That means thought has created the 'me', and the 'me' has apparently become independent of thought, and the 'me', being still part of thought, is the psychological structure. And perception can only take place when there is no 'me'.

DAVID BOHM: The 'me', this imaginary structure, is real as well, but the 'me' involves some sort of centre, doesn't it?

KRISHNAMURTI: Yes, of course. So there is a centre. Is that centre independent of thought?

DAVID BOHM: It would seem the centre *is* thought.

KRISHNAMURTI: That's it. That's why it is fragmented.

DAVID BOHM: Now you were saying that, because we think through the centre, there is going to be fragmentation.

KRISHNAMURTI: There must be. You see the basic reason for fragmentation is that we function from a centre.

DAVID BOHM: We think we function psychologically, from a centre. Physically we are forced to function from a centre because the body is the centre of our field of perception. Psychologically we form an imitation of that, we have the thought of the centre. That form is useful physically, but then it was extended psychologically.

KRISHNAMURTI: Right, that's why thought is fragmentary.

DAVID BOHM: Is there a thought which does not function from the centre? Or does it always have to?

KRISHNAMURTI: It has to. Because thought is memory from a centre.

DAVID BOHM: Let's try to explore that. Why does it have to be from a centre, why couldn't memory be without a centre? It's not clear to me why there cannot be just memory, just information.

KRISHNAMURTI: There can be information.

DAVID BOHM: Does that have to have a centre?

KRISHNAMURTI: If it's merely information, why should it have a centre?

DAVID BOHM: It's not clear to me why thought had to form a centre. We knew there was a centre but why did we give the centre such importance psychologically?

KRISHNAMURTI: Because thought never acknowledges to itself that it is mechanical.

DAVID BOHM: Thought was unable to acknowledge that it was mechanical. Why does that call for a centre? Thought not only creates the centre, but the idea of the centre was there, just for practical purposes. But thought used that idea for itself psychologically.

KRISHNAMURTI: Yes.

DAVID BOHM: Now why was it doing that?

KRISHNAMURTI: For a very simple reason. Thought said, 'I can't be mechanical, I must be something much more.'

DAVID BOHM: How does the centre make it more, then?

KRISHNAMURTI: Because the 'me' gives it a permanency.

DAVID BOHM: We should try to make it more clear that the centre gives this permanency in a lie.

KRISHNAMURTI: Thought has created this microphone. That is 'permanent', permanent in quotes.

DAVID BOHM: Relatively permanent, yes.

KRISHNAMURTI: And also thought created the 'me' as a permanent entity.

DAVID BOHM: Yes, but why did it pick on a centre to be permanent?

KRISHNAMURTI: Perhaps it picked it up because of the sun, which is the centre of the universe. And if there is a centre, as you said, it joins everything together.

DAVID BOHM: Yes, it gives unity.

KRISHNAMURTI: Unity, family and so on. But that centre becomes totally unnecessary when there is complete perception.

DAVID BOHM: It is necessary, you say, when there is *not* complete perception.

KRISHNAMURTI: It is not necessary, but that's what's happening.

DAVID BOHM: Not able to realize it is mechanical, thought began to treat its own products as living.

KRISHNAMURTI: That's right.

DAVID BOHM: And seeing their instability, their impermanence, it tried to establish something permanently and it found the centre useful for trying to do that. It is a form around which everything can be put and held together. Therefore, if everything is falling apart – if left to itself thought falls apart – if you establish a centre, it holds it all together.

KRISHNAMURTI: That's right, sir. So when you perceive something totally, the centre is non-existent. And yet, doesn't it bring in something? When you perceive something, doesn't that include everything? Isn't that the central thing that holds, that connects everything?

DAVID BOHM: To perceive?

KRISHNAMURTI: To perceive.

DAVID BOHM: The act.

KRISHNAMURTI: The act – *this is false*.

DAVID BOHM: Well, let's say something different, that the act of perception unites everything you know, and thought is imitating that by making a centre that unites everything and to the centre it attributes perception.

KRISHNAMURTI: That's right, as well as the observer, and so on.

DAVID BOHM: And also the thinker. It also attributes its own origin to that centre, and therefore it attributes truth to itself.

KRISHNAMURTI: That's right.

DAVID BOHM: And therefore life, and so on.

KRISHNAMURTI: Is there, sir, a perception of greed, of fear, and so on, or is there total perception which includes everything? You follow?

DAVID BOHM: Yes.

KRISHNAMURTI: So it isn't perception of greed, perception of belief, perception of organized religion.

DAVID BOHM: Let's say there is perception of *what is*.

KRISHNAMURTI: Yes. There is only perception.

DAVID BOHM: Now there is a question we might clear up. You said truth is that which is.

KRISHNAMURTI: Yes, there is only perception, not the perceiver.

DAVID BOHM: There is no perceiver, but perception is also that which is, isn't it?

KRISHNAMURTI: Yes, and the perceiver is the centre.

DAVID BOHM: Yes, thought attributes to the centre the quality of being a perceiver, as well as a thinker and an actor.

KRISHNAMURTI: All the rest of it – experiencer and so on.

DAVID BOHM: When thought has invented the centre, then it may attribute various qualities to that centre, such as thinking and feeling.

KRISHNAMURTI: That's right, sir.

DAVID BOHM: And if there is pain, or pleasure, it will attribute it to the centre. So therefore it becomes alive. Could you say that suffering arises when pain is attributed to the centre?

KRISHNAMURTI: Of course. As long as there is a centre there must be suffering.

DAVID BOHM: Yes, because when there is no centre then the pain is merely in thought.

KRISHNAMURTI: Merely physical.

DAVID BOHM: Either it's physical or it's memory – which is nothing.

KRISHNAMURTI: Yes, which is nothing.

DAVID BOHM: But if the memory of pain is attributed to the centre then it becomes real, apparently it might become something big.

KRISHNAMURTI: So we are seeing something; that is, if there is total perception, thought has no place in it.

DAVID BOHM: And that perception acts and thought may have a place in the action. That is what we were saying the other day.

KRISHNAMURTI: Yes. Now let's get this clear. There is total perception – in that there is no thought. And that perception is action.

DAVID BOHM: Yes, and that will change the quality of thought, like it is changing the brain cells.

KRISHNAMURTI: Yes, thought has only a mechanical function.

DAVID BOHM: By mechanical we mean, more or less, not intelligent; it's not creative, it's not intelligent.

KRISHNAMURTI: So if thought is merely mechanical, then it can operate mechanically in everything without any psychological centre, then there is no problem.

DAVID BOHM: I think even from the beginning, thought mistook itself for something living and creative and then it established the centre in order to make that permanent.

KRISHNAMURTI: Quite right. So, now we've seen why thought is fragmentary.

DAVID BOHM: But why is it fragmentary?

KRISHNAMURTI: Because of the centre. Thought created the centre as a permanency, and that centre forms a unit to pull everything together.

DAVID BOHM: Yes, the whole world is held together by the centre. Because if somebody feels his centre goes, he feels his whole world is going to pieces.

KRISHNAMURTI: That's right.

DAVID BOHM: So the centre is the same as the world.

KRISHNAMURTI: That's right, so thought is fragmentary.

DAVID BOHM: It doesn't quite explain why it is fragmentary.

KRISHNAMURTI: Because it has separated itself from the thing it has created.

DAVID BOHM: That's the point, so let's make that very clear. It has attributed to itself a centre which is separate from itself, whereas in fact it has created the centre and it is the centre.

KRISHNAMURTI: It *is* the centre.

DAVID BOHM: But it attributes to that centre the property of being alive and real, and so on. And that is a fragmentation.

KRISHNAMURTI: That's the basic thing.

DAVID BOHM: From there follows the necessity for the rest of the fragmentation of life. Because in order to maintain that those two are different, thought must then break up everything to fit that. And there enters the confusion, because either it separates things that are not separate, or it puts together things that are different.

In order to maintain the fiction that the centre is separate from thought, everything else has to be made to fit that.

KRISHNAMURTI: All existence has to be made to fit that centre.

DAVID BOHM: For example, if somebody attributes to the centre the quality of being a certain nation, then you must distinguish another nation as not belonging to this centre. So it fragments mankind in order to hold the centre together. Therefore the entire world is fragmented indefinitely, shattered into fragments.

KRISHNAMURTI: I want to get on to something else. If I perceive the nature of belief, it's finished. When there is total perception of fear, that's finished. And when there is total perception of greed, that's finished. Is that perception of one thing after the other, or is there total perception of the whole?

DAVID BOHM: If there were total perception of the whole, then what would there be left to do?

KRISHNAMURTI: That's what I want to find out. Is perception whole, and therefore it clears the entire field?

DAVID BOHM: Then what is there left to do?

KRISHNAMURTI: Wait, let's see if that is so. So it hasn't got to go through greed, belief, fear, pleasure – it has cleared the deck.

DAVID BOHM: Are you saying that man may perceive the whole nature of thought; or is it beyond that?

KRISHNAMURTI: Beyond that, a little more. Perception sees the nature of thought, and because it perceives the nature of thought, it perceives all the fragments.

DAVID BOHM: Yes, I see that. It brings up a question I wanted to ask for some time. In the book *Tradition and Revolution*, you mention the notion of essence, that perception distils the essence. Do you remember that?

KRISHNAMURTI: No, I don't remember, sorry.

DAVID BOHM: In some way there seemed to be a notion that there is perception – total perception being intelligence – and out of that came what you call the essence, it was distilled like a flower.

KRISHNAMURTI: Yes.

DAVID BOHM: Now, is that essence anything like this whole?

KRISHNAMURTI: That's what it is, of course. Now wait, I want to get this clear. Would you say there is no perception of fear, greed, envy, belief, but total perception of everything that thought has put together, and of the centre?

DAVID BOHM: Well, it's total. There's a phrase people sometimes use: 'essence and totality'.

KRISHNAMURTI: To perceive the essence and totality.

DAVID BOHM: Does that seem appropriate?

KRISHNAMURTI: I hesitate over the word 'essence'.

DAVID BOHM: So let's say you perceive the totality.

KRISHNAMURTI: Leave the word 'essence' for the moment. There is no partial seeing of greed, envy and all that, it is a total perception. And therefore total perception means seeing all the things that thought has put together, and it made itself a separate centre.

DAVID BOHM: We have to make it more clear now, because total may just mean all these things, or it may mean something else.

KRISHNAMURTI: To me it means something else. Total perception means to see thought attributing to itself certain qualities, thought creating the centre and giving to that centre certain attributes, and all the things arising from the psychological centre.

DAVID BOHM: That's the whole structure. That is what we often call the essence, the basic structure.

KRISHNAMURTI: Yes, if you call that 'essence', I agree.

DAVID BOHM: And that structure is universal. Would you agree that it's not just this thought or that thought, this problem or that problem?

KRISHNAMURTI: It is universal, yes. Now, is such a perception possible? You say that it *is* possible – nothing else. Because you tell me, I see that, I feel that, I see the truth of what you're saying. What you are saying is the truth; it's not mine or yours, it is the truth.

DAVID BOHM: *If* you say it is the truth, it's that which is.

KRISHNAMURTI: That which is actual.

DAVID BOHM: Yes, but it's both. I'm trying to get it a little more clear. When we say there is truth and there is actuality, the way we ordinarily use the word 'the actual' is really the right way for using the word 'individual'. It would seem to me the actuality is individual, it's undivided.

KRISHNAMURTI: Yes, individual, undivided.

DAVID BOHM: Actuality is undivided, but there is one moment of actuality or there may be another moment of actuality and so on. But when we see the essence, or when we see the totality, or the universal, then that includes all that.

KRISHNAMURTI: That's right.

DAVID BOHM: So that the truth goes beyond the individual, actual fact because it sees the total. It sees what is universal and necessary, the totality of the nature of thought. So that every individual example of thought is in there.

KRISHNAMURTI: That's right. When that is seen, thought is then merely mechanical.

DAVID BOHM: Then thought acknowledges it is mechanical.

KRISHNAMURTI: No, thought doesn't have to acknowledge it, it is mechanical.

DAVID BOHM: Yes, thought has changed, so that it is mechanical and ceases to consider itself to be non-mechanical. It occurred to me that if a man has to transform away from this conditioned existence, and if he is born conditioned, then there is no way out of it. From this conditioned mind there can be no way out. Therefore the only way out would be for somebody to come into existence who is not conditioned.

KRISHNAMURTI: Yes – proceed, yes.

DAVID BOHM: Therefore, if there is such a person, it is not the person who [or 'that'] is significant.

KRISHNAMURTI: Yes.

DAVID BOHM: It's just a part of the universal order. If you were to argue just for the sake of discussion, you could say that perhaps mankind has reached a stage where it is ready for a change.

KRISHNAMURTI: Yes, that's what they say.

DAVID BOHM: Many people have said that. But as you cannot change from the conditioned stage, it would be necessary to have...

KRISHNAMURTI: There must be a catalyst.

DAVID BOHM: ...a nucleus, which is unconditioned. That's the idea that occurred to me.

KRISHNAMURTI: To go back, if there is total perception of the nature of thought and all its activities, therefore there is the total perception of the content of consciousness. The content makes the consciousness, and all the rest of it, that used to be the centre. Total perception can only exist when the centre is not; then consciousness must be totally different.

DAVID BOHM: Yes. What would you say about its nature, then?

KRISHNAMURTI: What would be its nature? You see, sir, the centre, as you pointed out, is the factor of unification.

DAVID BOHM: It's the way people have always tried to unite.

KRISHNAMURTI: But it hasn't succeeded, ever. When the centre is not – which is perception of the totality of thought, and therefore the centre is not – consciousness must be something quite different.

DAVID BOHM: But the word 'consciousness' ordinarily would involve the idea of thought. Does it still continue?

KRISHNAMURTI: If there is no thought, there can't be consciousness.

DAVID BOHM: What do you call consciousness?

KRISHNAMURTI: Then, I said it must be something totally different. The consciousness which we have is with the centre, with all the content, with all the thought, with all that movement, and when there is total perception of *that*, that is not.

DAVID BOHM: The centre is not, and the whole order is different. Yes, and you also mentioned the brain cells, that it might involve the brain cells working in a different way.

KRISHNAMURTI: I think so.

DAVID BOHM: Or maybe different brain cells will work?

KRISHNAMURTI: I don't know, I think it works differently.
Sir, what is compassion? Is the centre capable of compassion?

DAVID BOHM: Well, I'd say the centre is not capable of anything real.

KRISHNAMURTI: No. Can the centre attribute compassion to itself?

DAVID BOHM: It certainly can do that.

KRISHNAMURTI: It can. Yes, as God, as anything; but if there is no attribution at all, then what is compassion? Is total perception compassion?

DAVID BOHM: Well, it has to be, to include the feeling for all.

KRISHNAMURTI: I should think one of the qualities of total perception is compassion.

DAVID BOHM: You see, the centre can only have feelings which are attributed to it, so it will have compassion for whatever it's identified with.

KRISHNAMURTI: Of course. I love you and I don't love others. Or I love others but I don't love you.

DAVID BOHM: It would have no understanding and therefore it would have no meaning.

KRISHNAMURTI: It's very interesting, this. How would you convey all this to somebody sentimental, romantic, wanting illusions, full of fanciful imaginations, with problems of sex, of fear? You tell him something and he won't even listen. Here we have the leisure to go into it; and we want to find out, because we're totally objective about ourselves.
I think that's where compassion comes in.

Gstaad, 25 July 1975

5   Tradition and truth

KRISHNAMURTI: What shall we start on?

DAVID BOHM: I think you said – as far as I can understand – that the thought process, if it is straight and healthy, may become aware of the action of truth and move in harmony with that. On the other hand, when the thought process is distorted and conditioned, it may not do that, but truth can actually act physically in the brain cells.

KRISHNAMURTI: Sir, would that be accurate?

DAVID BOHM: I don't know, we're trying to go into that.

KRISHNAMURTI: I think so, I feel that way.

DAVID BOHM: The brain is material. Matter exists, it has an actuality apart from thought, but we don't know it. We know only some of it, the complete depths of matter are unknown to us and perhaps will never be known, though we may know about it more and more. The brain, being made of matter, is constituted matter. We could never follow into the complete unknown depths in which thought arises in matter.

Thought has become conditioned over the ages, partly by heredity, and partly through tradition, culture and environment. It has been conditioned to self-deception, to falsify, to distort. And this is in the material structure of the brain. In one sense this conditioning constitutes a subtle kind of brain damage. Conditioning gives great importance to thought, to the self and to the centre. It overloads, it distorts and gradually damages the brain.

KRISHNAMURTI: Yes. Are you saying sir, that when the brain is overloaded by economic conditions, social environment...

DAVID BOHM: By fear and sorrow.

KRISHNAMURTI: ...by all the things that are going on in human beings, it does damage to the brain cells? I think that is so, that can be accepted.

DAVID BOHM: There is a real physical, chemical damage to the brain cells and those damaged brain cells will produce thought that is inherently distorted. Therefore, as thought tries to correct that damage, it does so from a distorted brain.

KRISHNAMURTI: Which makes it worse.

DAVID BOHM: Because it is distorted it must make it worse.

KRISHNAMURTI: Now, can there be a total perception which heals completely?

DAVID BOHM: The brain does not recognize this brain damage very clearly, but attributes it to something else. For example, it may attribute it to feeling uneasy, or else to some external circumstances. I think that a great deal of this damage to the brain happens through tradition. It occurred to me that tradition is a form of brain damage.

KRISHNAMURTI: I agree.

DAVID BOHM: Any tradition, good or bad, makes people accept a certain structure of reality, very subtly, without their realizing they are doing it, by imitation, or by example, or by words, just by statements. So very steadily the child builds up an approach in which the brain attributes things which are in the tradition to a reality which is independent of tradition. And it gives it tremendous importance. I think it's in every culture. Tradition has real effects of all sorts, which may even be valuable in some ways. But at the same time it conditions the brain to a certain view of reality, which is fixed.

In our culture we get a conditioning as to what is sensed to be real and necessary and right, what you have to make of your life, what sort of person you should be, what is really the right thing to do and so on. All this is picked up from tiny little indications. They don't seem to be thought, but seem to be the perception of reality. The brain treats thought as some reality independent of thought, and it becomes fragmented. A person may look at that reality and say, 'That's reality, I've got to keep my feet on the ground.' But this ground has been created by tradition, by thought; it is no ground, it has nothing under it at all. It is sustained and nourished by this damaged brain, which is unable to get out of that circle.

Culture also has certain values which cannot be discarded, and one of the dangers that could arise in an uncritical look at what you say, is that somebody might want to discard culture because it's not clear.

KRISHNAMURTI: Sir, what does that word 'culture' mean? To cultivate?

DAVID BOHM: It is based on 'cultivate'.

KRISHNAMURTI: That is 'to grow'. So we mean by culture that which grows, that which is capable of growth. What benefit is given by culture?

DAVID BOHM: Science, art, music, literature and technology. Every culture has a certain technology with which it approaches reality; certain methods have been developed to live, to grow things, to make things.

KRISHNAMURTI: Has thought created culture? Of course it has.

DAVID BOHM: Some culture seems to be necessary for man to survive.

KRISHNAMURTI: I wonder if it is necessary.

DAVID BOHM: Perhaps it isn't, but at least it appears to be.

KRISHNAMURTI: Let's question it. I think there is a danger of depending on it, of using it as a means to go beyond, to achieve, or penetrate into something else.

Culture is growth from childhood to adulthood. Sir, is there some part of the brain which is untouched by culture, by anything?

DAVID BOHM: That is a question which science couldn't consider at present. It's beyond anything anybody could do because we don't know what that would mean, from the material point of view. If we say there is a certain material structure to the brain, it is impossible to tell whether it is touched by culture or not, because at present our way of looking at it is too crude.

KRISHNAMURTI: If I say something about it, will you listen? – not discard it, not throw it out?

We said that consciousness is its content. If that content can be emptied – emptied in the sense of being no longer conditioned – is there a part of the brain where neither tradition, nor time, where nothing has made an imprint on it?

DAVID BOHM: Do you think it's some particular part of the brain?

KRISHNAMURTI: Not only a particular part of the brain, but a particular consciousness which is not *this* consciousness.

DAVID BOHM: Another consciousness, are you saying?

KRISHNAMURTI: Another consciousness.

DAVID BOHM: Which may be another function. Or is it another part? What are you saying?

KRISHNAMURTI: No, let me get it clear. My brain is conditioned by tradition, culture and heredity.

DAVID BOHM: That means it is damaged in some way.

KRISHNAMURTI: It was damaged, and it has healed itself completely.

DAVID BOHM: You say it was damaged and healed itself.

KRISHNAMURTI: Suppose my brain healed itself and now it is unconditioned.

DAVID BOHM: But how can it heal itself if it is damaged?

KRISHNAMURTI: Through having an insight or a perception which is not the perception of the damaged brain.

DAVID BOHM: I understand. We'll say the brain is not damaged through and through; there is a certain damage to the brain, but there is still a function that is not damaged.

KRISHNAMURTI: That's right. And is there a consciousness which is totally different from the conditioned consciousness, which operates, say, when a really great composer has that perception?

DAVID BOHM: Let's take Beethoven, who was deaf but who had a perception. We know his brain was damaged, he was often very disturbed mentally. And yet you say there was a part of his brain, or a function, or something which could work despite that damage.

KRISHNAMURTI: If he was really damaged, he couldn't have been a musician.

DAVID BOHM: But would you say in general that damage, even cultural damage, is not deep. It may appear deep but perhaps it isn't.

KRISHNAMURTI: Yes, I think it is not too deep.

DAVID BOHM: Yes, it works on a certain level.

KRISHNAMURTI: My brain is damaged by tradition but I can step out of it. The brain says 'rubbish'...

DAVID BOHM: The damage is in certain functions of the brain which are based on memory.

KRISHNAMURTI: ...and it can put that aside.

DAVID BOHM: Memory is not really a deep function of the brain, though it may appear so. It may treat itself as deep, attribute depth to itself.

KRISHNAMURTI: If I'm a Catholic and I talk with you, and you show me the fault of it, I reason and I see it. Then it's finished, I'm out of it, I'm no longer a Catholic.

DAVID BOHM: In principle I think this is right. What actually happens is that a person may see this in a flash of insight, but a certain part of the damaged brain attributes to itself the property of being very deep and beyond thought, and therefore it escapes this insight. It doesn't mean that the damage is deep, but that the damaged part attributes to itself great depth. So that often it is not enough merely to explain to a person who is a Catholic; he might see it in that moment but...

KRISHNAMURTI: Wait a minute. Say, for instance, I'm attached to my wife, or to something else. You point it out, and because I respect you I listen. If I am fairly sensitive to what you are saying, then it's finished, it's over, I am not attached any more.

DAVID BOHM: It doesn't commonly happen that way.

KRISHNAMURTI: Why?

DAVID BOHM: That's what we want to find out. One reason is that this conditioning attributes to itself some significance which is very deep and beyond mere memory and thought. Suppose I have been brought up in the Catholic tradition. I have been exposed to it non-verbally and very thoroughly and it has left all sorts of marks. Then when I become frightened, once again it all seems real. And therefore I forget what you said.

KRISHNAMURTI: Of course. But, sir, that's too easy.

DAVID BOHM: But that is what actually happens.

KRISHNAMURTI: I think there is something deeper than that. Let's go into it a little, it may not be.

I listen to you because you are serious, because you have detached yourself. When you show it to me and say, 'Look, listen', because I respect you, I am attentive. What you say has a tremendous meaning and I see the truth of it – not the rationalization, but the truth of what you are saying.

DAVID BOHM: But there is the tremendous tendency in this traditional conditioning to resist that truth.

KRISHNAMURTI: I am *not* resisting it, because, first of all, I want transformation, that is a basic necessity for me as a human being.

DAVID BOHM: Yes, but then there is the other necessity of security, which we have discussed.

KRISHNAMURTI: You show me truth and transformation. There is tremendous security. You point out to me that if I transform myself totally, I will be eternally safe and secure. Because you have seen it, because you have got it, then when you say something it's a shock, and I see it. But if I haven't transformed, if I am a crook, a phoney, then whatever you say has no meaning for me.

DAVID BOHM: Then how do you account for the fact that you've been talking for so many years and it has had...?

KRISHNAMURTI: I think, sir, basically, people won't listen.

DAVID BOHM: Yes, but then let's come back to the same point: why not?

KRISHNAMURTI: Because I don't think people are interested.

DAVID BOHM: Why not?

KRISHNAMURTI: Why should they be interested?

DAVID BOHM: Because life is such a mess.

KRISHNAMURTI: They have their little harbours in which they are sheltering themselves.

DAVID BOHM: But that's an illusion.

KRISHNAMURTI: *You* say it is an illusion, *to me* it is not.

DAVID BOHM: I know, but why does the brain resist seeing this illusion? Very often people get shocks which show that something is wrong and then they go back.

KRISHNAMURTI: Of course.

DAVID BOHM: We have to get through this tendency to go back. We listen to the person who really sees, and there is a shock, but maybe the brain will then go back later.

KRISHNAMURTI: You are asking why it goes back. That's very simple – because of habit, because of tremendous years of tradition.

DAVID BOHM: The only answer which is adequate is one that will stop that. As I see it, an explanation which doesn't end this thing is not a full explanation.

KRISHNAMURTI: Does explanation end it?

DAVID BOHM: It doesn't, but you just explained it by saying it was habit.

KRISHNAMURTI: I can say it is habit, and we can go back and forth. But what makes me break the habit and [so] brings about a total seeing in the damaged brain?

DAVID BOHM: So that it will see and not go back.

KRISHNAMURTI: Sir, when a man sees that organization of any spiritual movement is useless, he drops it instantly, he never goes back to it, never cultivates it, never organizes it again. Now what has taken place in that man? He perceives the truth of it.

DAVID BOHM: Yes, but you have said that particular man was not actually deeply conditioned in the first place. Now we have to consider another man, who was deeply conditioned. There is the man who was not deeply conditioned who sees the falseness of organized pursuit of truth, and he drops it. That's fairly easy because the conditioning was never very deep.

KRISHNAMURTI: But the other man's conditioning is much stronger and he may temporarily see it and then go back.

DAVID BOHM: Can that man be given a shock? At other times you've said shocks are no use.

KRISHNAMURTI: I know, I'm just asking. I can shock you but you go back tomorrow.

DAVID BOHM: I'll go back but it may work for a while.

KRISHNAMURTI: So what is the thing that makes me see something and end it and not go back? You see, sir, people haven't been able to do this, they say it's only for the few, that many cannot change.

DAVID BOHM: Perhaps the brains have been damaged too much in the past. You don't accept that?

KRISHNAMURTI: I don't quite, that's too easy. What makes you see something and it's finished? I don't see it, but you point it out and then I see it for a few months or on some days, and suddenly it disappears and I'm back.

DAVID BOHM: I think it's more likely a gradual slipping back into the old habit.

KRISHNAMURTI: What is the thing that makes it?

(Pause)

Sir, is attention a conscious process?

DAVID BOHM: We can say it's not. It may be this unconscious which we talked about.

KRISHNAMURTI: If it is not a conscious or unconscious process, that is, not a process of time, not a process of thought, is there another kind of attention which acts and it's over? I'm just trying to find out.

DAVID BOHM: Would you say, as we said before, that it's something beyond attention that acts?

KRISHNAMURTI: Yes, that is what I'm trying to get at. If you tell me to rationalize my attachments, my reactions, my defences, and so on, I listen rationally, logically, and it's still within the field of thought. And within the field of that thought, whatever thought does, it cannot produce a permanent radical transformation.

You have explained to me rationally, and you say, 'That is not enough, you won't change if you remain there, you'll go back to it.' And you point out to me, you say, 'Look, don't think, don't rationalize, just listen to me, don't control, don't resist, just listen.' You are not appealing to the rational, thoughtful process, you are appealing to something that is beyond thought, beyond my usual consciousness. You are appealing to something much deeper in me, you are touching something which has nothing to do with the movement of thought. Would that be right? You are appealing to me at a level of which I am not conscious. You are appealing to me at a level which may be called compassion – which is not on the level of thought. If you appeal to me at that level I can't go back to the former habits. Is that possible?

Sir, is love the factor of profound change? Not all the movements of thought and all the explanations, all the pros and cons.

DAVID BOHM: Would you say it is truth? Previously you said it was truth. Is there a distinction?

KRISHNAMURTI: No, of course not, it's the whole thing. Truth is love, compassion and everything else. I just want to see if that is so. Can you, out of your compassion, out of your love, touch something in me that transforms me, because to you there is that truth, you see truth as something... And you live in that, you have that feeling of something immense. And from that you speak, and you say, 'My friend, you have tried to do it for fifty years and you haven't done it.' To that the ordinary answer would be that the brain is too damaged, there are very few brains which are not damaged, perhaps you can affect them. So we go back to saying 'Only a few', and all the rest of it. But that is not a complete answer.

DAVID BOHM: One view would be that only a few can change and that this would spread, or something like it. You are not accepting that?

KRISHNAMURTI: No. That is going back into culture, into time, back into the whole business of tradition. Again this will bring new damage – this is what actually takes place.

DAVID BOHM: Are you saying that if we are using culture in order to bring order to the mind, this will damage the brain? But then what can we use culture for?

KRISHNAMURTI: Now, just a minute. What shall we do? You speak out of the depths of that something which is immense and I listen to you, and you affect me at that level. It is a temporary affair, and I go back to my old damage. You have not healed me completely, only partially and the old damage takes over.

Or are you talking to me at such depth that the very listening is healing completely? Why doesn't it happen? You tell me, very clearly, 'Don't be attached', and you explain it to me and your explanation comes out of the compassion, out of the perception of truth. And I see it, I have an insight into it, but I lose that insight.

DAVID BOHM: I think that maybe there is some clue in the nature of the brain damage, in what it does in so far as it distorts perception. The whole thing depends on clear perception. This brain damage can produce what appears to be perception, what it takes to be perception.

KRISHNAMURTI: But you are appealing from something much greater. And I respond to it for a few days or a few months and then it's gone. Or I say, 'Please remind me of it, let me read books and keep on memorizing them'. And I lose it. Why is it, sir? We come back to the same thing. Is it that my brain is not only damaged, but refuses to see anything new because whatever you say might lead me to some danger?

DAVID BOHM: The brain attributes danger to seeing. Something happens in which the brain projects danger into that situation. It is thought, but it comes back as if it were something seen.

KRISHNAMURTI: So you talk about fear, about pleasure, about suffering, and you say, 'Look, please listen to me; for God's sake, out of your heart listen to me.' I listen to you, but I go back.

DAVID BOHM: It is also the culture which continually brings it back. In any relationship within this cultural frame of reality, that frame of thought is already there.

KRISHNAMURTI: Quite. How does this operate? Are you appealing to me, talking to my daily unconscious consciousness? Are you showing me that in that consciousness there is no answer? Are you talking to me at that level, or are you talking to me, not only at that level, but also at a much deeper level? It may be that I am not used to that deep level.

DAVID BOHM: It could be.

KRISHNAMURTI: I think, sir, that's more like it. I've always gone to the well with a little bucket. And you say, 'Look, that little bucket won't do anything, it will quench your thirst only momentarily.' So you are not talking to me at the level I am used to. You are talking to me at a deeper level, which I am not used to. And I get used to it while you are talking to me but the moment you stop talking it's gone.

DAVID BOHM: It goes in time, either at that moment or later.

KRISHNAMURTI: So is it, sir, that the brain wants to reduce everything to habit? I see what you say at a deep level. And I reduce that, or make it into a habit and therefore I lose it. And you tell me at that deep level, 'There is no time, there is no habit, you can't capture it by your brain; your brain will make it into a habit, into a tradition, into another damage. Don't do that.'

DAVID BOHM: Thought tends to accompany everything that happens, and it gives an imitation, an accompaniment like music which builds up and that becomes the habit. Then thought takes that habit for the same as the original. At the beginning thought says the accompaniment is helping; later it mistakes that accompaniment for the thing itself.

KRISHNAMURTI: Yes, but you tell me, 'See the whole structure, be tremendously aware of it.'

DAVID BOHM: It seems to be part of our tradition that there should be some thought, that thought should not stop. In fact, every tradition must demand that thought doesn't stop.

KRISHNAMURTI: Of course, quite right, every tradition is that.

DAVID BOHM: Children are brought into a tradition; when they follow it, everybody says, 'That's right, you are good', and so on. Tradition goes back to that feeling of belonging to the family and to the community, of being approved of because you are not only doing what they say, what you're supposed to do, but believing what you are supposed to believe, and believing in what is real. This tradition includes the belief that we have a correct consensus as to what is real, a belief that we don't create our reality. Now, if you say we're going to talk at this deep level...

KRISHNAMURTI: It goes against all that.

DAVID BOHM: And that begins in very subtle ways to start working.

KRISHNAMURTI: Just a minute. Can you speak from that depth to me? And I don't even talk about it, I have an insight into it, I feel it, but can I sustain it?

DAVID BOHM: Man's old tradition was mystery, then came the modern tradition of rationality, of being free of every form of tradition.

KRISHNAMURTI: That's what you're asking me. You say, 'Look, there is every form of tradition.'

DAVID BOHM: At first sight one would say one can't do it, because one feels culture gives one the chance to think and look at these things.

KRISHNAMURTI: It gives you safety, security, a place in the community.

DAVID BOHM: Also it gives you order in the mind, and so on. The point is that all of this is the result of damage, somehow it is a distortion due to the damaged brain. I think that's the firmest point I can see.

KRISHNAMURTI: You have explained to me all that. Verbally, intellectually, in every way you have made it perfectly clear to me. Fear, no place in society, no security – all that is involved if I leave tradition.

DAVID BOHM: Yes. Distortion causes the readiness to believe whatever will make me feel better, and so on.

KRISHNAMURTI: All that. And you say, 'I'm not talking to that, because then one is merely going round and round in circles.' You are not talking to me at that level at all, you are talking to me at a level which is not this.

DAVID BOHM: You say that is the function of the part of the brain that is not conditioned, that is not damaged.

KRISHNAMURTI: I don't know. But there is a depth which is not touched by the traditional brain, by the damaged brain, by the brain which is conditioned, a depth, a dimension, which is not touched by thought. All you have said about tradition, everything, is the process of thought, and that process of time has not touched this. You have talked to me, you have shown it to me, and if there is an action from that, the brain can never be damaged again. It may be that your talking to me at that level heals the brain completely.

DAVID BOHM: You were saying last time that there is a direct action on the matter of the brain.

KRISHNAMURTI: I think there is something in this.

DAVID BOHM: Now is this the only way? Does it depend on somebody having a brain that is not conditioned and who can talk from that depth?

KRISHNAMURTI: Naturally, if you are healthy you can talk to me.

DAVID BOHM: But if there were only conditioned people then they would never find a way out.

KRISHNAMURTI: Absolutely. How can the damage be healed?

DAVID BOHM: It goes against the modern tradition to say that, even against some of what you say: that we must observe and discover and find our way out. If the brain were not damaged, it could obviously do that, but being damaged it cannot do it.

KRISHNAMURTI: But you realize it cannot do it. Therefore you stop.

DAVID BOHM: But you were the one who was not damaged, who communicated this from another depth.

KRISHNAMURTI: Yes. Wait. I realize through your talks, through reading – it doesn't matter how I realize it – that the damaged brain, whatever it does, will still be in that area.

DAVID BOHM: Yes. But there is the tendency of this damaged brain to come to conclusions and present them as facts.

KRISHNAMURTI: Therefore I realize all the tricks of the damaged brain.

DAVID BOHM: One of the tricks is to say that nothing can be done, or, 'I'll keep on working on it.'

KRISHNAMURTI: Yes, quite. I don't know if you saw on television last night, a young man was singing folk songs and thousands of people were listening. It is another way than science.

DAVID BOHM: You mean that was another attempt of the brain to heal itself in a false way?

KRISHNAMURTI: To escape. It can't do anything socially, it can't do anything morally, it can't do anything scientifically, it can't do anything artistically, at least it can go and listen to this nonsense going on. Of course if the brain is completely damaged it can't do anything.

DAVID BOHM: One has to look at it carefully. If something has been damaged materially, perhaps it can never be repaired – we don't know.

KRISHNAMURTI: If it is completely damaged, you can't do anything about it, you are ready for an asylum. But we are talking of a brain that is not too damaged.

DAVID BOHM: You cannot know whether the damage can be healed or not.

KRISHNAMURTI: Now wait. You explain all this, and you say that whatever the damaged brain does, which is the result of thought and tradition and all the rest of it, will produce further damage. So because you point it out I realize that. That is the first necessity, that I realize it. Then, after I've realized it, you talk to me at a depth which thought has not touched.

My question is, once having had an insight into that depth, why should I be caught and go back into the old field? If you have pointed out that depth and I have an insight into it and I perceive that depth, can I ever go back to the other? Will not what you say act as a tremendous shock, or a tremendous jolt?

DAVID BOHM: The brain may get used to any shock or jolt.

KRISHNAMURTI: Therefore I have to be very clear about the structure of thought. Otherwise the depth becomes the habit. Because I am very serious, very concerned, through your pointing out to me the whole activity of thought, it comes to a stop. And the feeling of the depth can never become a habit. If depth becomes habit it becomes pleasure, tradition, fear of losing it and all that. Now is that depth within consciousness?

DAVID BOHM: Before, you said there is another kind of consciousness.

KRISHNAMURTI: That's right, it's not in that consciousness. It's not in the area of thought. Thought cannot capture it.

DAVID BOHM: Would you say there is this other consciousness which is still a function of the brain? Do you mean it's going on in the brain?

KRISHNAMURTI: Not if you say 'brain' in the sense that it is the product of time, the product of evolution, and so on.

DAVID BOHM: I don't know whether it's the product of time or not. If you say nature is continually changing, it's cultivated, it's growing, wouldn't you say there is a creation in nature as well? Would you say nature is the product of time?

KRISHNAMURTI: It is and it's not, surely.

DAVID BOHM: That is what we are trying to get hold of. It may solve the problem of the brain too, because the brain has arisen in the same way as other natural things.

KRISHNAMURTI: Yes. Or is it cultivated carefully?

DAVID BOHM: If we take the evolution of all sorts of plants and animals, in one sense it seems to happen in time.

KRISHNAMURTI: Yes, it seems to have taken time.

DAVID BOHM: I don't know if you would agree entirely with that, you say it has and it hasn't.

KRISHNAMURTI: I'm just asking myself. I suppose it has in one sense, hasn't it? So the brain is not only the product of culture and time, but isn't there also something, part of the brain, which is not of time?

DAVID BOHM: That's what we want to come to, because there is a structure of the brain which has evolved through time, and that structure may go beyond thought. For example, it may involve attention, awareness.

KRISHNAMURTI: I see what you are trying to say. You are saying, 'The brain evolves in time, and in that time there is awareness, attention.'

DAVID BOHM: Beyond thought, beyond culture, and not thought.

KRISHNAMURTI: It is still within that area of time.

DAVID BOHM: At least the brain which is able to give attention to something took time to evolve.

KRISHNAMURTI: Yes, but is there an attention which is not of time?

DAVID BOHM: That is the question: is there? The attention itself may not be of time.

KRISHNAMURTI: The attention itself is not of time.

DAVID BOHM: The ability, the structure of the brain which is able to have attention, depended on time.

KRISHNAMURTI: The capacity, yes, but attention itself is not of time.

DAVID BOHM: But it may be taking place in the brain, though it is not of time.

KRISHNAMURTI: That's right. Yes, attention itself is out of time, but the capacity to have attention may involve time.

DAVID BOHM: Yes, it involves growth, culture, and also you have said that as the brain grows older it grows more mature, its capacity in some way improves. That seems to involve time. So therefore in some way time is involved to produce a certain capacity.

KRISHNAMURTI: Capacity means time.

DAVID BOHM: But something may happen within that capacity, which is not of time. In some sense it depends on growth; the young child has a different capacity.

KRISHNAMURTI: So we are saying growth is time, time is necessary, but attention is not in time.

DAVID BOHM: And truth is not, compassion is not.

KRISHNAMURTI: None of that is in time.

DAVID BOHM: And that compassion, or truth, may operate on the material structure of the brain, so the brain is changed physically; even its time and behaviour are different, something new is introduced into time.

KRISHNAMURTI: That's right.

DAVID BOHM: Can we get more clear on creation? Because creation means, literally, to cause to grow, and you have said perception is creation.

KRISHNAMURTI: Yes. Perception is cause to grow?

DAVID BOHM: Is it?

KRISHNAMURTI: No.

DAVID BOHM: Creativity is perception, but we have to clarify what is meant, because ordinarily the very word 'creation' means to cause to grow, and we can say nature is creative because it causes new species to grow, and so on. Now in what sense is man creative? Let's say Beethoven had an insight and this gave rise to new music, so in that sense it caused new music to grow. But I want to be more clear about creation.

KRISHNAMURTI: But, sir, the depth which produced the music, that depth is not of time.

DAVID BOHM: No, but couldn't we say that perhaps even in nature there is that depth which brings about something which is not of time? The mechanical explanation of nature is only limited, it won't cover everything. The creation of new forms in nature may also depend on what is beyond time.

KRISHNAMURTI: Maybe. But a human being can see for himself that compassion is out of time, truth is out of time, and the depth from which that compassion comes is out of time. And therefore it is not cultivable.

DAVID BOHM: No, it cannot be made to grow. So we say the origin, the essence of creativity, does not grow, but creativity may cause something to grow in the field of time. Is that right?

KRISHNAMURTI: Yes, that's quite right.

DAVID BOHM: Because that is what we had in mind, that the new perception should cause the growth of a new society, a new man. But creativity itself in essence does not grow, it is not created.

KRISHNAMURTI: That's right. But out of that which is not created there can be a new man, a new society.

DAVID BOHM: This creates a new brain that is not damaged.

KRISHNAMURTI: To go back to the point: why do I lose it? I have insight into that profound truth and it's lost after a time. Or it's not lost at all but becomes empty because all my tradition says, 'Hold on to it, make it into a habit.' How subtle all this is.

DAVID BOHM: Yes, it says, 'Make it into another tradition.'

KRISHNAMURTI: That's right. Sir, die to everything that thought has built as creation, as tradition. You see, you speak from that depth, and I listen to you and you explain all the movements of thought as time. That I understand very easily. And you say, 'Thought, time, must come to a stop, otherwise there is no depth.' So I hunger after it, I practise – all the rest of that rubbish goes on. But if I listen to you and see, not the rationalization, but the truth of what you say – the truth being the total perception of what you say – I can only do that against all the pressures of tradition, against everything that says, 'Don't do this.'

Gstaad, 6 August 1975

Part II

Seeing the illusions of security

6 The liberation of insight

KRISHNAMURTI: We have asked what is the origin of all human movement. Is there an original source, a ground from which all this – nature, man, the whole universe – sprang? Is it bound by time? Is it in itself complete order, beyond which there is nothing more?

And we have talked about order, whether the universe is based on time at all, and whether man can ever comprehend and live in that supreme order. We want to investigate, not merely intellectually but also profoundly, how to comprehend and live, move from that ground, that ground that is timeless, and beyond which there is nothing. Can we go on from there?

I don't know if, as a scientist, you will agree that there is such a ground, or that man can ever comprehend it, live in it; not in the sense that he is living in it, but that itself is living? Can we as human beings come to that?

DAVID BOHM: I don't know if science as it is now constituted can say much about that.

KRISHNAMURTI: Science doesn't talk about it but would you, as a scientist, give your mind to the investigation of that?

DAVID BOHM: Yes, I think that implicitly science has always been concerned with trying to come to this ground, but to attempt it by studying matter to the greatest possible depth, of course, is not enough.

KRISHNAMURTI: Didn't we ask if a human being, living in this world that is in such turmoil, can be in absolute order first, as the universe is in absolute order, and comprehend an order which is universal?

DAVID BOHM: Yes.

KRISHNAMURTI: I can have order in myself, by careful observation, self-study, self-investigation, and understanding the nature of disorder. The very insight of that understanding dispels disorder. That's one level of order.

DAVID BOHM: Yes, that's the level that most of us have been concerned with till now, you see. We see this disorder going on in the world and in ourselves, and we say it is necessary to be aware of it and to observe it and, as you say, to dispel it.

KRISHNAMURTI: But that's a very small affair.

DAVID BOHM: Yes, but we agreed that people generally don't feel it is a small affair. They feel that clearing up the disorder in themselves and the world would be a very big thing, and perhaps all that is necessary.

KRISHNAMURTI: But I am referring to the fairly intelligent, knowledgeable and cultured human being, 'cultured' meaning civilized. He can, with a great deal of enquiry and investigation, come to the point when he can bring order in himself.

DAVID BOHM: Then some people would say, if only we could bring that order into the whole of society.

KRISHNAMURTI: Well, we will, if human beings are all tremendously orderly in that inward sense, perhaps create a new society. But that again is a very small affair.

DAVID BOHM: I understand that, but I feel we should go into it carefully because people commonly don't see it as small. Only a few have seen that there's something beyond that.

KRISHNAMURTI: Much more beyond that.

DAVID BOHM: Perhaps it might be worth thinking about why it is not enough to go into the order of man and society, just to produce orderly living. In what sense is that not enough?

KRISHNAMURTI: Because we live in chaos, we think that to bring order is a tremendous affair, but in itself it isn't. I can put my room in order, so that it gives me certain space, certain freedom; I know where things are, I can go directly to them. That's a physical order. Can I put things in myself in order, which means not to have conflict, not to have comparison, not to have any sense of 'me' and 'you' and 'they', everything that brings about such division, out of which grows conflict? That's simple. If I'm a Hindu and you are a Muslim, we are eternally at war with each other.

DAVID BOHM: Yes, and in every community people fall apart in the same way.

KRISHNAMURTI: All society breaks up that way, but if one understands that, and profoundly realizes it, it's finished.

DAVID BOHM: Suppose we say we have achieved that, then what? I think some people might feel it's so far away that it doesn't interest them. They might say, wait till we achieve it before we worry about the other.

KRISHNAMURTI: All right, sir, let's start again. I'm in disorder, physically and psychologically. Around me the society in which I live is also utterly confused. There is a great deal of injustice; it is a miserable affair. I can see that very simply. I can see that my generation and past generations have contributed to this. And I can do something about it. That's simple. I can say, well, I'll put my house in order. The house is myself and it must be in order before I can move further.

DAVID BOHM: But suppose somebody says, 'My house is not in order'?

KRISHNAMURTI: All right, my house is in disorder. Then let me put it in order, which is fairly simple. If I apply my mind and my heart to the resolution of that, it's fairly clear. But we don't want to do that. We find it tremendously difficult because we are so bound to the past, to our habits and our attitudes. We don't seem to have the energy, the courage, the vitality, to move out of it.

DAVID BOHM: What's not simple is to know what will produce that energy and courage. What will change all this?

KRISHNAMURTI: I think that what will change all this is to have an insight into it.

DAVID BOHM: The key point seems to be that, without insight, nothing can change.

KRISHNAMURTI: Will insight really alter the whole structure and nature of my being? That is the question, isn't it?

DAVID BOHM: What seems to be implied is that, if we look at a rather small question like the order of daily life, it will not involve our whole being.

KRISHNAMURTI: No, of course not.

DAVID BOHM: And therefore the insight will be inadequate.

KRISHNAMURTI: Yes, it's like being tied to something, to a belief, to a person, an idea, some habit, some experience. That inevitably must create disorder, because being tied implies dependence, the escape from one's own loneliness, fear. Now total insight into that attachment clears it all away.

DAVID BOHM: Yes. I think we are saying that the self is a centre creating darkness or clouds in the mind, and insight penetrates that. It could dispel the clouds so that there would be clarity and the problem would vanish.

KRISHNAMURTI: That's right, vanish.

DAVID BOHM: But that would take a very intense, total insight.

KRISHNAMURTI: That's right, but are we willing to go through that? Or is our attachment or tie to something so strong that we're unwilling to let go? That is the case with most people. Unfortunately, it's only the very few who want to do this kind of thing.

Now, can insight wipe away, banish, dissolve the whole movement of being tied, attached, dependent, lonely, with one blow as it were? I think it can. I think it happens when there is profound insight. That insight is not merely the movement of memory, knowledge, experience; it is totally different from all that.

DAVID BOHM: It is insight into the whole of disorder, into the source of all disorder of a psychological nature.

KRISHNAMURTI: It is all that.

DAVID BOHM: With that insight the mind can clear up, and then it would be possible to approach the cosmic order.

KRISHNAMURTI: That's what I want to get at. That's much more interesting than this. Any serious man must put his house in order. And that must be complete order, order in the whole of man, not order in a particular direction. The particular resolution of a particular problem is not the resolution of the whole.

DAVID BOHM: The key point is that finding the source, the root that generates the whole, is the only way.

KRISHNAMURTI: Yes, that's right.

DAVID BOHM: Because, if we try to deal with a particular problem, it's still always coming from the source.

KRISHNAMURTI: The source is the 'me'. That little source, little pond, little stream, apart from the great source, must dry up.

DAVID BOHM: Yes, the little stream confuses itself with the great one, I think.

KRISHNAMURTI: Yes, we're not talking about the great stream, the immense movement of life, we're talking about the little 'me' with the little movement, little apprehensions and so on, that is creating disorder. As long as that centre, which is the very essence of disorder, is not dissolved, there is no order.

So at that level it is clear. Can we go on from there? Now, is there another order totally different from this? This is man-made disorder, and therefore man-made order. The human mind, realizing that and seeing the disorder that it can bring about in itself, then begins to ask if there is an order that is totally different, of a dimension which it is necessary to find, because this man-made order is such a small affair.

I can put my house in order. All right. Then what? Perhaps if many of us do it, we'll have a better society. That is admitted, relevant, necessary, but it has its limitation. Now, a human being who has really deeply understood the disorder made by human beings and its effect on society asks, 'Is there is an order that is beyond all this?' The human mind isn't satisfied with merely physical order. That has limitations, boundaries, so he says, 'I've understood that, let's move.'

DAVID BOHM: How do we get into that question? Even in science, men seek the order of the universe looking to the end or the beginning or to the depth of its structure. Many have sought the absolute, and the word 'absolute' means free of all limitation, all dependence, all imperfection. The 'absolute' has been the source of tremendous illusion, of course, because the limited self seeks to capture the absolute.

KRISHNAMURTI: Of course, that's impossible. So how do we approach this? How do we answer this question? As a scientist, would you say there is an order which is beyond all human order and disorder?

DAVID BOHM: Science is not able to say anything because any order discovered by science is relative. Not knowing what to do, men have felt the need for the absolute, and not knowing how to get it they have created the illusion of it in religion and in science or in many other ways.

KRISHNAMURTI: So what shall I do? As a human being who is the totality of human beings, there is order in my life. That order is naturally brought about through insight and so perhaps it will affect society. Move from that. The enquiry then is, is there an order that is not man-made? Let's put it that way. I won't even call it absolute order.

Man has sought a different dimension and perhaps used the word 'order'. He has sought a different dimension, because he has understood this dimension. He has lived in it, he has suffered in it, he has gone through all kinds of mess and misery and he has come to the end of all that. Not just verbally, but he has actually come to the end of all that. You may say there are very few people who do that, but this question must be put.

How does the mind approach this problem? I think man has struggled to find this out, sir. All so-called religious people – the mystics, the saints, with their illusions – have attempted to grasp this. They have tried to understand something which is not all this.

Does it come about through, if I may use the word, 'meditation', as measure?

DAVID BOHM: The original meaning of the word 'meditation' is to measure, to ponder, to weigh the value and significance. Perhaps that may have meant that such a measurement would only have significance for seeing that there is disorder.

KRISHNAMURTI: That's what I would say, that measurement can exist only where there is disorder. We are using the word 'meditation' not as 'measure' or even 'to ponder or think over', but as meditation that is the outcome of bringing order in the house, and moving from there.

DAVID BOHM: So if we see things are in disorder in the mind, then what is meditation?

KRISHNAMURTI: First the mind must be free of measurement. Otherwise it can't enter into the other. All *effort* to bring order into disorder is disorder.

DAVID BOHM: So we are saying that it is the attempt to control that is wrong; we see that it has no meaning. And now we say there's no control. What do we do?

KRISHNAMURTI: No, no, no. If I have an insight into the whole nature of control, which is measure, that liberates the mind from that burden.

DAVID BOHM: Yes. Could you explain the nature of this insight, what it means?

KRISHNAMURTI: Insight is not a movement from knowledge, thought, remembrance, but the cessation of all that to look at the problem with pure observation, without any pressure, without any motive, to observe the whole movement of measurement.

DAVID BOHM: Yes, I think we can see that measurement is the same as becoming and the attempt of the mind to measure itself, to control itself, to set itself a goal, is the very source of the disorder.

KRISHNAMURTI: That is the very source of disorder.

DAVID BOHM: In a way that was the wrong way of looking at it, a wrong turning, when man extended measurement from the external sphere into the mind.

KRISHNAMURTI: Yes.

DAVID BOHM: But now the first reaction would be that if we don't control this thing it will go wild. That's what someone might fear.

KRISHNAMURTI: Yes, but you see, if I have an insight into measurement, that very insight not only banishes all movement of measurement, but there is a different order. It doesn't go wild; on the contrary.

DAVID BOHM: It does not go wild because it has begun in order. It is really the attempt to measure it that makes it go wild.

KRISHNAMURTI: Yes, that's it. The measurement becomes wild; it is confusion.

Now let's proceed. After establishing all this, can the mind, through meditation – using the word 'meditation' without any sense of measurement, comparison – find an order, a state where there is something that is not man made? I've been through all the man-made things and they are all limited; there is no freedom in them, there is chaos.

DAVID BOHM: When you say you've been through man-made things, what are they?

KRISHNAMURTI: Religion, worship, prayers, science, anxieties, sorrow, attachment, detachment, loneliness, suffering, confusion, ache, all that.

DAVID BOHM: Also all the attempts by revolution.

KRISHNAMURTI: Of course, physical revolution, psychological revolution. Those are all man made. And also so many people have put this question, and then they say, 'God'. That is another concept, and that very concept creates disorder.

Now, one has finished with all that. Then the question is: is there something beyond all this that is never touched by human thought, mind?

DAVID BOHM: Yes, now that makes a difficult point: not touched by the human mind, but mind might go beyond thought.

KRISHNAMURTI: Yes, that's what I want.

DAVID BOHM: Do you mean by the mind only thought, feeling, desire, will, or something much more?

KRISHNAMURTI: For the time being we have said the human mind is all that.

DAVID BOHM: But it's not; the mind is now considered to be limited.

KRISHNAMURTI: No. As long as the human mind is caught in that, it is limited.

DAVID BOHM: Yes, the human mind has potential.

KRISHNAMURTI: Tremendous potential.

DAVID BOHM: Which it does not realize now when it is caught in thought, feeling, desire, will, and that sort of thing.

KRISHNAMURTI: That's right.

DAVID BOHM: Then we'll say that which is beyond this is not touched by this limited sort of mind.

KRISHNAMURTI: Yes.

(Pause)

DAVID BOHM: Now what will we mean by the mind which is beyond this limit?

KRISHNAMURTI: First of all, sir, is there such a mind? Is there such a mind that actually, not theoretically or romantically, can say, 'I've been through this'?

DAVID BOHM: You mean, through the limited stuff.

KRISHNAMURTI: Yes. And being through it means finished with it. Is there such a mind? Or does it only think it has finished with it, and therefore it creates the illusion that there is something else? I won't accept that. A human being, a person, 'X', says, 'I have understood this. I have seen the limitation of all this. I have been through it, and I have come to the end of it. And this mind, having come to the end of it, is no longer the limited mind.' Is there a mind which is totally limitless?

DAVID BOHM: What is the relation between that limited mind and the brain?

KRISHNAMURTI: I want to be clear on this point. This mind, brain, the whole of it, the whole nature and the structure of the mind includes the emotions, the brain, the reactions, physical responses, all that. This mind has lived in turmoil, in chaos, in loneliness, and it has understood all that, has had a profound insight into it. Having such a deep insight cleared the field. This mind is no longer that mind.

DAVID BOHM: Yes, it's no longer the original mind.

KRISHNAMURTI: Yes. Not only that, no longer the limited mind, the damaged mind. Damaged mind means damaged emotions, damaged brain.

DAVID BOHM: The cells themselves are not in the right order.

KRISHNAMURTI: Quite. But when there is this insight and therefore order, the damage is undone.

DAVID BOHM: By reasoning you can see it's quite possible, because you can say the damage was done by disorderly thoughts and feelings, which over-excite the cells and disrupt them and now with the insight, that stops and there is a new process.

KRISHNAMURTI: Yes, it's like a person going for fifty years in a certain direction. If he realizes suddenly that it's the wrong direction, the whole brain changes.

DAVID BOHM: It changes at the core and then the wrong structure is dismantled and healed. That may take time.

KRISHNAMURTI: That's right.

DAVID BOHM: But the insight...

KRISHNAMURTI: Is the factor that changes.

DAVID BOHM: And that insight does not take time.

KRISHNAMURTI: That's right.

DAVID BOHM: But it means that the whole process has changed the origin.

KRISHNAMURTI: The limited mind with all its consciousness and its content says it is over. Now is that mind – which has been limited but has had insight into its limitation and moved away from that limitation – an actuality? Is it then something that is really tremendously revolutionary? And therefore it is no longer the human mind?

When the human mind with its consciousness, which is limited, is ended, then what is the mind?

DAVID BOHM: Yes, and what is the person, what is the human being?

KRISHNAMURTI: What is a human being, then? And then what is the relationship between that mind, which is not man made, and the man-made mind? Can one observe, really, deeply, without any prejudice whether such a mind exists? Can the mind, conditioned by man, uncondition itself so completely that it's no longer man made? Can the man-made mind liberate itself completely from itself?

DAVID BOHM: Yes, of course that's a somewhat paradoxical statement.

KRISHNAMURTI: Of course it's paradoxical; but it's actual, it is so. Let's begin again. One can observe that the consciousness of humanity is its content. And its content is all the man-made things – anxiety, fear and so on. And it is not only the particular, it is the general. Having had an insight into this, it has cleansed itself from that.

DAVID BOHM: Well, that implies that it was always potentially more than that, but insight enabled it to be free of that. Is that what you mean?

KRISHNAMURTI: I won't say that insight is potential.

DAVID BOHM: There is a little difficulty of language if you say the brain or the mind had an insight into its own conditioning and then you're almost saying it became something else.

KRISHNAMURTI: Yes, I am saying that, I am saying that. The insight transforms the man-made mind.

DAVID BOHM: Yes, but then it's no longer the man-made mind.

KRISHNAMURTI: It's no longer. That insight means the wiping away of all the content of consciousness. Not bit by bit by bit; the totality of it. And that insight is not the result of man's endeavour.

DAVID BOHM: Yes, but then that seems to raise the question of where it comes from.

KRISHNAMURTI: All right. Where does it come from? Yes. In the brain itself, in the mind itself.

DAVID BOHM: Which, the brain or the mind?

KRISHNAMURTI: Mind, I'm saying the whole of it.

DAVID BOHM: We say there is mind, right?

KRISHNAMURTI: Just a minute, sir. Let's go slowly. It's rather interesting. Consciousness is man made, general and particular. And logically, reasonably one sees the limitations of it. Then the mind has gone much further. Then it comes to a point when it asks, 'Can all this be wiped away at one breath, one blow, one movement?' And that movement is insight, the movement of insight. It is still in the mind, but it's not born of that consciousness.

DAVID BOHM: Yes. Then you are saying the mind has the possibility, the potential, of moving beyond that consciousness.

KRISHNAMURTI: Yes.

DAVID BOHM: The brain, mind can do that, but it hasn't generally done it.

KRISHNAMURTI: Yes. Now, having done all this, is there a mind which is not only not man made, but that man cannot conceive, cannot create, that is not an illusion? Is there such a mind?

DAVID BOHM: Well, I think what you are saying is, this mind having freed itself from the general and particular structure of the consciousness of mankind, from its limits, is now much greater. Now you say that this mind is raising a question.

KRISHNAMURTI: This mind is raising the question.

DAVID BOHM: Which is what?

KRISHNAMURTI: Which is, first, is that mind free from the man-made mind? That's the first question.

DAVID BOHM: It may be an illusion.

KRISHNAMURTI: Illusion is what I want to get at. One has to be very clear. No, it is not an illusion, because he sees measurement is an illusion; he knows the nature of illusion; that it is born of desire. And illusions must create limitation, and so on. He has not only understood it, he's over it.

DAVID BOHM: He's free of desire.

KRISHNAMURTI: Free of desire. That is his nature. I don't want to put it so brutally. Free of desire.

DAVID BOHM: It is full of energy.

KRISHNAMURTI: Yes. So this mind, which is no longer general and particular, is therefore not limited; the limitation has been broken down through insight, and therefore the mind is no longer that conditioned mind. Now, then, what is that mind? Being aware that it is no longer caught in illusion?

DAVID BOHM: Yes; but we were saying it raised a question about whether there is something much greater.

KRISHNAMURTI: Yes, that's why I'm raising the question. Is there a mind which is not man made? And if there is, what is its relationship to the man-made mind?

You see, every form of assertion, every form of verbal statement is not that. So we're asking if there is a mind which is not man made. I think that can only be asked when the limitations are ended, otherwise it's just a foolish question.

So one must be absolutely free of all this. Then only can you put that question. Then you put that question – not 'you' – then the question is raised: is there a mind that is not man made, and if there is such a mind, what is its relationship to the man-made mind? Now, is there such a mind? Of course there is. Of course, sir. Without being dogmatic or personal, or all that business, there is. But it is not God, we've been through all that.

There is. Then, the next question is, what is the relationship of that to the human mind, man-made mind? Has it any relationship? Has this relationship to that? Obviously not. The man-made mind has no relationship to that. But that has a relationship to this.

DAVID BOHM: Yes, but not to the illusions in the man-made mind.

KRISHNAMURTI: Let's be clear. My mind is the human mind. It has illusions, desires and so on. And there is that other mind which has not, which is beyond all limitations. This illusory mind, the man-made mind, is always seeking that.

DAVID BOHM: Yes, that's its main trouble.

KRISHNAMURTI: Yes, that's its main trouble. It is measuring, it is 'progressing', saying 'I am getting nearer, going farther'. And this mind, the human mind, the mind that's made by human beings, the man-made mind, is always seeking that, and therefore it's creating more and more mischief, confusion. This man-made mind has no relationship to that.

Now, has that any relationship to this?

DAVID BOHM: I was suggesting that it would have to have, but that if we take the illusions which are in the mind, such as desire and fear and so on, it has no relationship to those, because they are figments anyway.

KRISHNAMURTI: Yes, understood.

DAVID BOHM: But that can have a relationship to the man-made mind in understanding its true structure.

KRISHNAMURTI: Are you saying, sir, that that mind has a relationship to the human mind the moment it's moving away from the limitations?

DAVID BOHM: Yes, but in understanding those limitations it moves away.

KRISHNAMURTI: Yes, moves away. Then that has a relationship.

DAVID BOHM: We have to get the words right. The mind that is not limited, that is not man-made, cannot be related to the illusions that are in the man-made mind.

KRISHNAMURTI: No, agreed.

DAVID BOHM: But it has to be related to the source, as it were, to the real nature of the man-made mind, which is behind the illusion.

KRISHNAMURTI: The man-made mind is based on what?

DAVID BOHM: Well, on all these things we have said.

KRISHNAMURTI: Yes, which is its nature. Therefore, how can that have a relationship to this, even basically?

DAVID BOHM: The only relationship is in understanding it, so that some communication would be possible, which might communicate to the other person.

KRISHNAMURTI: No, I'm questioning that.

DAVID BOHM: Yes, because you were saying that the mind that is not man made may be related to the limited mind and not the other way round.

KRISHNAMURTI: I even question that.

DAVID BOHM: Yes, all right, you are changing that.

KRISHNAMURTI: No, I'm just pushing it a little.

DAVID BOHM: It may or may not be so, is that what you mean by questioning it?

KRISHNAMURTI: Yes, I'm questioning it. What is the relationship then of love to jealousy? It has none.

DAVID BOHM: Not to jealousy itself, no; that is an illusion, but...

KRISHNAMURTI: I'm taking two words, say 'love' and 'hatred'. Love and hatred really have no relationship to each other.

DAVID BOHM: No, not really. I think that one might understand the origin of hatred, you see.

KRISHNAMURTI: Ah, yes, yes. I see. You're saying that love can understand the origin of hatred and how hatred arises. Does love understand that?

DAVID BOHM: Well, I think that in some sense it understands its origin in the man-made mind, and that having seen the man-made mind and all its structure and moved away...

KRISHNAMURTI: Are we saying, sir, that love – using that word for the moment – has a relationship to non-love?

DAVID BOHM: Only in the sense of dissolving it.

KRISHNAMURTI: I'm not sure, I'm not sure, we must be awfully careful here. Or the ending of itself...

DAVID BOHM: Which is it?

KRISHNAMURTI: With the ending of hatred, the other is; the other has no relationship to the understanding of hatred.

DAVID BOHM: We have to ask how it gets started then, you see.

KRISHNAMURTI: Suppose I have hatred. I can see the origin of it: it's because you insulted me.

DAVID BOHM: That's a superficial notion of the origin. Why one behaves so irrationally is the deeper origin. There's nothing real if you merely insult me, so why should I respond to the insult?

KRISHNAMURTI: Because all my conditioning is that.

DAVID BOHM: Yes, that's what I mean by your understanding the origin.

KRISHNAMURTI: But does love help me to understand the origin of hatred?

DAVID BOHM: No, but I think that someone in hatred, moving, understands the origin and moves away.

KRISHNAMURTI: Moving away, then the other is. The other cannot help the movement away.

DAVID BOHM: No, but suppose one human being has this love and another has not. Can the first one communicate something which will start the movement in the second one?

KRISHNAMURTI: That means 'Can A influence B?'

DAVID BOHM: Not influence, but, for example, why should anybody be talking about any of this?

KRISHNAMURTI: That's a different matter. No, the question, sir, is: is hate dispelled by love?

DAVID BOHM: No.

KRISHNAMURTI: Or, in the understanding of hatred and the ending of it, the other is?

DAVID BOHM: That's right. But say that here in A the other now is, that A has reached that. Love is for A, and he sees B, and we're asking what he is going to do. You see, that's the question. What is he going to do?

KRISHNAMURTI: What is the relationship between the two? My wife loves, and I hate. She can talk to me, she can point out to me my unreasonableness, and so on, but her love is not going to transform the source of my hatred.

DAVID BOHM: That's clear, yes, except love is the energy which will be behind the talk.

KRISHNAMURTI: Behind the talk, yes.

DAVID BOHM: The love itself doesn't sort of go in there.

KRISHNAMURTI: Of course not, that's romantic.

So the man who hates, who has an insight into the source of it, the cause of it, the movement of it, and ends it, has the other.

DAVID BOHM: Yes. We say A is the one who has seen all this and he now has the energy to put it to B. It's up to B what happens.

KRISHNAMURTI: Of course. I think we had better pursue this.

Brockwood Park, 14 September 1980

7 The intelligence of love

KRISHNAMURTI: We have been saying that a human being who has worked his way through all the problems of life both physical and psychological, and has really grasped the full significance of freedom from psychological memories and conflicts and travails, comes to a point where the mind finds itself free but hasn't gathered that supreme energy needed to go beyond itself.

Can the mind, brain, the whole psychological structure, ever be free from all conflict, from all shadow of any disturbance? Or is the idea of complete freedom an illusion?

DAVID BOHM: That's one possibility. Then some people would say we could have partial freedom.

KRISHNAMURTI: Or is the human condition so determined by the past, by its own conditioning, that it can never free itself from it, as some philosophers have stated?

There have been some deeply non-sectarian religious people, totally free from all organized religions and beliefs, rituals, dogmas, who have said it can be done, but very few have said it. Or some say it will take a very long time, that you must go through various lives and suffer all kinds of miseries and ultimately you come to that. But we are not thinking in terms of time. We are asking if a human being – granting, knowing that he is conditioned, deeply, profoundly, so that his whole being is that – can ever free himself. And if he can, what is beyond? That's what we were coming to.

Would that question be reasonable or valid unless the mind has really finished with all the travail of life? We said our minds are man-made and asked if there is a mind that is not man made? Is it possible that the man-made mind can free itself from its own man-made mechanical mind? How shall we find this out?

DAVID BOHM: There's a difficult thing to express here. If this mind is totally man made, totally conditioned, then in what sense can it get out of it? If you say that it had at least the possibility of something beyond...

KRISHNAMURTI: Then it becomes a reward, a temptation.

DAVID BOHM: Logically it may appear to be inconsistent to say that the mind is totally conditioned and yet it's going to get out.

KRISHNAMURTI: If one admits that there is a part that is not conditioned, then we enter into quite another thing.

DAVID BOHM: That may be another inconsistency.

KRISHNAMURTI: Yes. We have been saying that the mind, although deeply conditioned, can free itself through insight. That is the real clue to this. Would you agree to that?

DAVID BOHM: Yes.

KRISHNAMURTI: We went into what the nature of insight is. Can insight uncondition the mind completely and wipe away completely all the illusions, all the desires? Or is it partial?

DAVID BOHM: If we say the mind is totally conditioned it suggests something static, which would never change. Now, if we say the mind is always in movement, then it seems in some way it becomes impossible to say what it is at this moment. We couldn't say it has been totally conditioned.

KRISHNAMURTI: No, let's say I'm totally conditioned; it's in movement, but the movement is within a border, within a certain field. And the field is very definitely marked out. The mind can expand it and contract it, but the boundary is very, very limited, definite. Now, it is always moving within that limitation. Can it die away from that?

DAVID BOHM: That's the point; that's another kind of movement. It's kind of in another dimension, I think you've said.

KRISHNAMURTI: Yes. And we say it is possible through insight, which is also a movement, a totally different kind of movement.

DAVID BOHM: Yes, but then we say that movement does not originate in the individual nor in the general mind.

KRISHNAMURTI: Yes. It is not the insight of the particular or the general. We are then stating something quite outrageous.

DAVID BOHM: That rather violates most of the sort of logic that people use. Either the particular or the general should cover everything, in terms of ordinary logic.

KRISHNAMURTI: Yes.

DAVID BOHM: Now, if you're saying there's something beyond both, this is already a question which has not been stated, and I think it has great importance.

KRISHNAMURTI: How do we then state it, or how do we then come to it?

DAVID BOHM: People divide themselves roughly into two groups. One group feels the ground is the concrete, particular daily activity. The other group feels that the general, the universal, is the ground. One is the more practical type, and the other the more philosophical type. In general, this division has been visible throughout history, and also in everyday life, wherever you look.

KRISHNAMURTI: But, sir, is the general separate from the particular?

DAVID BOHM: It's not. Most people agree with that, but people tend to give emphasis to one or the other. Some give emphasis to the particular, saying the general is there but if you take care of the particular the general will be all right. The others say the general is the main thing, the universal, and by getting that right you'll get the particular right. So there's been a kind of imbalance to one side or the other, a bias in the mind of man. What's being raised here is the notion that it is neither the general nor the particular.

KRISHNAMURTI: That's right. That's just it. Can we discuss it logically? Using your expertise, your scientific brain and this man who is not all that, can we have a conversation to find out if the general and particular are one, not divided at all?

So where are we now? We are neither the particular nor the general. That's a statement that can hardly be accepted reasonably.

DAVID BOHM: Well, it's reasonable if you take thought to be a movement rather than a content. Then thought is the movement between the particular and the general.

KRISHNAMURTI: Thought is a movement. Quite; we agree to that. But thought is the general and thought is the particular.

DAVID BOHM: Thought is also the movement. In the movement it goes beyond being one or the other.

KRISHNAMURTI: Does it?

DAVID BOHM: Well, it can. Ordinarily it does not, because ordinarily thought is caught on one side or the other.

KRISHNAMURTI: That's the whole point, isn't it? Ordinarily the general and the particular are in the same area.

DAVID BOHM: Yes, and you fix on one or the other.

KRISHNAMURTI: Yes, but in the same area, in the same field. And thought is the movement between the two. Thought has created both.

DAVID BOHM: Yes, it has created both and moves between.

KRISHNAMURTI: Yes, between and around and in that area. And it has been doing this for millenniums.

DAVID BOHM: Yes, and most people would feel that's all it can do.

KRISHNAMURTI: Yes. Now we are saying that, when thought ends, that movement which thought has created also comes to an end. Therefore time comes to an end.

DAVID BOHM: We should go more slowly here, because you see it's a jump from thought to time. We've gone into it before but it's still a jump.

KRISHNAMURTI: Sorry, right. Let's see. Thought has created the general and the particular, and thought is a movement that connects the two. Thought moves round it, so it is still in the same area.

DAVID BOHM: Yes, and doing that it has created time, which is part of the general and the particular. Time is a particular time and also a general time.

KRISHNAMURTI: Yes, but you see, thought is time.

DAVID BOHM: Well that's another question. We have said that thought has a content which is about time, and that thought is a movement which is time. It could be said to be moving from the past into the future.

KRISHNAMURTI: But, sir, thought is based on time, thought is the outcome of time.

DAVID BOHM: Yes, but then does that mean that time exists beyond thought? If you say thought is based on time, then time is more fundamental than thought.

KRISHNAMURTI: Yes.

DAVID BOHM: We have to go into that. You could say that time is something which was there before thought, or at least is at the origin of thought.

KRISHNAMURTI: Time is there when there is the accumulation of knowledge.

DAVID BOHM: Well, that has come out of thought to some extent.

KRISHNAMURTI: No, I act and learn. That action is not based on previous knowledge, but I do something, and in the doing I learn.

DAVID BOHM: Yes, then that learning is registered in the memory.

KRISHNAMURTI: Yes, so is not thought essentially the movement of time?

DAVID BOHM: We have to say in what sense this learning is the movement of time. You can say that when we learn it is registered, and then that what you have learned operates in the next experience.

KRISHNAMURTI: Yes. The past is always moving to the present.

DAVID BOHM: Yes, and mixing, confusing with the present. And the two together are again registered as the next experience.

KRISHNAMURTI: So are we saying time is different from thought, or time is thought?

DAVID BOHM: We are saying this movement of learning, and the response of memory into experience and then registering, is time, and that is also thought.

KRISHNAMURTI: Yes, that is thought. Is there a time apart from thought?

DAVID BOHM: That's another question. Would we say that physically or in the cosmos time has a significance apart from thought?

KRISHNAMURTI: Physically, yes, I understand that.

DAVID BOHM: So then we're saying in the mind or psychologically.

KRISHNAMURTI: Psychologically. As long as there is psychological accumulation as knowledge, as the 'me', and so on, there is time. It is based on time.

DAVID BOHM: Wherever there is accumulation there is time.

KRISHNAMURTI: Yes, that's the point. Wherever there is accumulation there is time.

DAVID BOHM: Which turns the thing around, because usually you say time is first and in time you accumulate.

KRISHNAMURTI: No, I would put it round the other way, personally.

DAVID BOHM: Yes. But it's important to see that it's put the other way. Then we'd say, suppose there is no accumulation, then what?

KRISHNAMURTI: Then – that's the whole point – there is no time. As long as I am accumulating, gathering, becoming, there is the process of time. But if there is no gathering, no becoming, no accumulation, where does psychological time exist? So thought is the outcome of psychological accumulation, and that accumulation, that gathering, gives it a sense of continuity, which is time.

DAVID BOHM: It seems it's in movement. Whatever has been accumulated is responding to the present, with the projection of the future and then that is again registered. Now the accumulation of all that's registered is in the order of time, one time, the next time, and so on.

KRISHNAMURTI: That's right. So we're saying, thought is time. Psychological accumulation is thought and time.

DAVID BOHM: We're saying that we happen to have two words when really we only need one.

KRISHNAMURTI: One word. That's right.

DAVID BOHM: Because we have two words we look for two things.

KRISHNAMURTI: Yes. There is only one movement, which is time and thought, time plus thought, or time/thought. Now, can the mind, which has moved for millenniums in that area, free itself from that?

DAVID BOHM: Yes, now, why is the mind bound up? Let's see exactly what's holding the mind.

KRISHNAMURTI: Accumulation.

DAVID BOHM: Yes, but why does the mind continue to accumulate?

KRISHNAMURTI: Because in accumulation there is apparent safety, there is apparent security.

DAVID BOHM: The accumulation of physical food may provide a certain kind of security. And then since no distinction was made between the outer and the inner, there was the feeling that one could accumulate inwardly either experiences or some knowledge of what to do.

KRISHNAMURTI: Are we saying the outward physical accumulation is necessary for security, and that same movement, same idea, same urge, moves into the field of the psychological, so we accumulate there hoping to be secure?

DAVID BOHM: Yes, inwardly hoping to accumulate pleasant memories, or relationships, or things you could count on, principles you could count on.

KRISHNAMURTI: So psychological accumulation is the illusion of safety, protection, security?

DAVID BOHM: Yes. It does seem that the first mistake was that man never understood the distinction between what he has to do outside and what he has to do inside.

KRISHNAMURTI: It is the same movement, outer and inner.

DAVID BOHM: The movement that was right outwardly man carried inward, without knowing that that would make trouble.

KRISHNAMURTI: So where are we now? A human being realizes all this, has come to the point when he says, 'Can I really be free from this accumulated security and thought and psychological time?' Is that possible?

DAVID BOHM: Well, if we say that it had this origin, then it should be possible to dismantle it, but, if it were built into us, nothing could be done.

KRISHNAMURTI: Of course not. It is not built into us.

DAVID BOHM: Most people act as though they believe it was.

KRISHNAMURTI: Of course, that's absurd.

DAVID BOHM: If it's not built into us, then the possibility exists for us to change. Because in some way it was built up in the first place through time.

KRISHNAMURTI: If we say it is built in, then we are in a hopeless state.

DAVID BOHM: Yes, and I think that's one of the difficulties of people who use evolution. They're hoping by bringing in evolution to get out of this static boundary. They don't realize that evolution is the same thing; or that it's even worse, it's the very means by which the trap was made.

KRISHNAMURTI: Yes. So, as a human being, I have come to that point. I realize all this, I'm fully aware of the nature of this. And my next question is: can this mind move on from this field altogether, and enter, perhaps, into a totally different dimension? And we said it can only happen when there is insight.

DAVID BOHM: It seems that insight arises when one questions this whole thing very deeply, and sees it doesn't make sense.

KRISHNAMURTI: Yes. Now, having had insight into this and seen its limitation, and looking beyond it – what is there beyond?

DAVID BOHM: It's very difficult to even bring this into words, but we said something has to be done on this line.

KRISHNAMURTI: Yes. I think it has to be put into words.

DAVID BOHM: Could you say why? Because many people might feel we should leave this entirely non-verbal.

KRISHNAMURTI: Can we say the word is not the thing? Whatever the description, it is not the real, not the truth, however much you embellish or diminish it. We recognize that the word is not that, then what is there beyond all this? Can my mind be so desireless that it won't create an illusion, something beyond?

DAVID BOHM: Then it's a question of desire; desire must be in this time process.

KRISHNAMURTI: Desire is time. Being, becoming, is based on desire.

DAVID BOHM: They are one and the same, really.

KRISHNAMURTI: Yes, one and the same. Now, when one has an insight into that whole movement of desire, and its capacity to create illusion, it's finished.

DAVID BOHM: Since this is a very crucial point, we should try to say a little more about desire: how it's intrinsic in the accumulating process, how it comes out in many different ways. For one thing you could say that, as you accumulate, there comes a sense of something missing. You feel you should have more, something to complete it. Whatever you have accumulated is not complete.

KRISHNAMURTI: Yes. Could we go into the question of becoming, first? Why is it that all human beings have this urge to become? We can understand it outwardly, simply enough. Physically, you develop a muscle to make it stronger. You can find a better job, have more comfort, and so on. But why is there this need in the human mind to try to become enlightened – let's use that word for the moment – trying to become more good, better?

DAVID BOHM: There must be a sense of dissatisfaction with what's there already. A person feels he would like to be complete. Suppose, for example, he has accumulated memories of pleasure, but these memories are no longer adequate and he feels something more is needed.

KRISHNAMURTI: Is it dissatisfaction, is that it?

DAVID BOHM: Well, wanting to get more. Eventually he feels that he must have the whole, the ultimate.

KRISHNAMURTI: I'm not at all sure whether the word 'more' is not the real thorn. More: I will be more; I will have more; I will become; this whole movement of moving forward, gaining, comparing, advancing, achieving – psychologically.

DAVID BOHM: The word 'more' is just implicit in the whole meaning of the word 'accumulate'. So if you're accumulating you have to be accumulating more, there's no other way to do it.

KRISHNAMURTI: So why is there this need in the human mind?

DAVID BOHM: Well, we didn't see that this 'more' is wrong, inwardly. If we started outwardly to use the term 'more', but then carried it inward, for some reason we didn't see how destructive it was.

KRISHNAMURTI: Why? Why haven't fairly intelligent philosophers and religious people, who have spent a great part of their lives achieving, seen this very simple thing? Why haven't the intellectuals seen the simple fact that where there is accumulation there must be more?

DAVID BOHM: They've seen that but they don't see any harm in it.

KRISHNAMURTI: I'm not sure they see it.

DAVID BOHM: They are trying to get more, so they say, 'We are trying to have a better life.' For example, the Nineteenth Century was the 'century of progress'. Men were improving all the time.

KRISHNAMURTI: Outward progress.

DAVID BOHM: But they felt that man would be improving himself inwardly too.

KRISHNAMURTI: But why haven't they ever questioned this?

DAVID BOHM: What would make them question it?

KRISHNAMURTI: This constant struggle for the more.

DAVID BOHM: They thought that was necessary for progress.

KRISHNAMURTI: But is that progress? Has that same outward urge to be better moved into the psychological realm?

DAVID BOHM: Can we make it clear why it does harm in the psychological realm?

KRISHNAMURTI: Let's think it out. What is the harm in accumulating, psychologically? Oh yes, it divides.

DAVID BOHM: What does it divide?

KRISHNAMURTI: The very nature of accumulation brings about a division between you and me, and so on.

DAVID BOHM: Could we make that clear, because it is a crucial point? I can see that you are accumulating in your way and I accumulate in my way. Then we try to impose a common way of accumulating and that's conflict. They say everybody should be 'more'.

KRISHNAMURTI: That is impossible. That never takes place. I have accumulated psychologically as a Hindu; another has accumulated as a Muslim; there are thousands of divisions. Therefore accumulation in its very nature divides people, and therefore creates conflict.

So can we say, then, that in accumulation man has sought psychological security, and that security with its accumulation is the factor of human division psychologically? That's why human beings have accumulated, not realizing its consequences. Realizing that, is it possible not to accumulate?

Suppose my mind is filled with this process of occupation, which is psychological knowledge. Can all that end? Of course it can.

DAVID BOHM: If the mind can get to the root of it.

KRISHNAMURTI: Of course it can. It sees that it is an illusion that in accumulation there is security.

DAVID BOHM: But we are saying that desire is what keeps people going on with it.

KRISHNAMURTI: Not only desire but this deep-rooted instinct to accumulate, for the future, for safety. That and desire go together. So desire plus accumulation is the factor of division, conflict. Now, I'm asking, can that end? If it ends through an action of will, it is still the same thing.

DAVID BOHM: That's part of desire.

KRISHNAMURTI: Yes. If it ends because of punishment or reward, it's still the same thing. So the mind, one's mind, sees this and puts all that aside. But does the mind become free of accumulation? Yes, sir, I think it can; that is, have no psychological knowledge as accumulation at all.

DAVID BOHM: Yes, I think that we have to consider that knowledge goes very much further than is ordinarily meant. For example, if you're getting knowledge of a microphone, you build up an image, a picture of the microphone and everything goes into that and one expects it to continue. So if you have knowledge of yourself, it builds up a picture of yourself.

KRISHNAMURTI: Can one have knowledge of oneself?

DAVID BOHM: No, but if you think you have, if one thinks that there is knowledge about what sort of person you are, that builds up into a picture, with the expectations.

KRISHNAMURTI: But, after all, if you have knowledge of yourself, you have built an image already. But once you realize psychological accumulation as knowledge is an illusion and destructive and causes infinite pain and misery, it is finished.

DAVID BOHM: I know certain things in knowledge, and that it's foolish to have that kind of knowledge about myself, but then there may be other kinds of knowledge which I don't recognize as knowledge.

KRISHNAMURTI: What kind, what other kinds of knowledge does one have? Preferences, likes and dislikes, prejudices, habits. All that is in the image that one has created.

DAVID BOHM: Yes. Now, man has developed in such a way that that image seems extraordinarily real, and therefore its qualities don't seem to be knowledge.

KRISHNAMURTI: All right, sir. So, we have said accumulation is time and accumulation is security, and where there is psychological accumulation there must be division. And thought is the movement between the particular and the general, and thought is also born out of the image of what has been accumulated. All that is one's inward state. That is deeply embedded in me. I recognize it is somewhat necessary physically. But how do I set about realizing that psychologically it is not? How do I, who have had the habit of accumulating for millenniums, general and particular, not only recognize the habit, but, when I do recognize the habit, how does that movement come to an end? That is the real question.

Where does intelligence play a part in all this?

DAVID BOHM: There has to be intelligence to see this.

KRISHNAMURTI: Is it intelligence? Is it so-called ordinary intelligence, or some other intelligence, something entirely different?

DAVID BOHM: I don't know what people mean by intelligence, but if they mean just merely the capacity to...

KRISHNAMURTI: To discern, to distinguish, to solve technical problems, economic problems and so on, I would call that partial intelligence because it is not really...

DAVID BOHM: Yes, call that 'skill in thought'.

KRISHNAMURTI: All right, skill in thought. Now wait a minute, that's what I'm trying to find out. I realize the reason for accumulation, division, security, the general and particular, thought. I can see the logic of all that. But logic, reason and explanation don't end the thing. Another quality is necessary. Is that quality intelligence? I'm trying to move away from 'insight' for a while. Is intelligence associated with thought? Is it related, is it part of thought, is it the outcome of very clear precise, exact, logical, conclusions of thought?

DAVID BOHM: That would still be more and more skill.

KRISHNAMURTI: Yes, skill.

DAVID BOHM: Yes, but when we say intelligence, at least we suggest the intelligence has a different quality.

KRISHNAMURTI: Yes. Is that intelligence related to love?

DAVID BOHM: I'd say they go together.

KRISHNAMURTI: Yes, I'm just moving slowly to that. You see, I've realized all that we have discussed, and I've come to a blank wall, a solid wall that I can't go beyond. And in observing, looking, fishing around, I come upon this word 'intelligence'. And I see that the so-called intelligence of thought, skill, is not intelligence. So I'm asking further if this intelligence is associated with, or related to, or part of, love. One cannot accumulate love.

DAVID BOHM: No, people might try. People do try to guarantee love.

KRISHNAMURTI: It sounds silly! That is all romantic nonsense, cinema stuff. You cannot accumulate love. You cannot associate it with hate. That love is something entirely different. And has that love intelligence? Which then operates? Which then breaks down the wall?

All right, sir, let's begin again. I don't know what that love is. I know all the physical bit. I realize pleasure, desire, accumulation, remembrance, images, are not love. I realized all that long ago. But I've come to the point where this wall is so enormous that I can't even jump over it. So I'm now fishing around to see if there is a different movement which is not a man-made movement. And that movement may be love. I'm sorry to use that word because it has been so spoilt and misused, but we'll use it for the time being.

So is that love, with its intelligence, the factor that will break down or dissolve or break up this wall? Not 'I love you', or 'you love me'. It's not personal or particular. It's not general or particular. It is something beyond. I think when one loves with that intelligence it covers the whole, it's not the particular or general. It is that. It is light; it's not particular light. If that is the factor that will break down the wall that is in front of me, then I don't know that love. As a human being, having reached a certain point, I can't go beyond it to find that love. What shall I do? Not 'do' or 'not do', but what is the state of my mind when I realize that any movement this side of the wall is still strengthening the wall? I realize, through meditation or whatever you do, that there is no movement, but the mind can't go beyond it.

But you come along and say, 'Look, that wall can be dissolved, broken down, if you have that quality of love with intelligence.' And I say, 'Excellent, but I don't know what it is.' What shall I do? I can't do anything, I realize that. Whatever I do is still on this side of the wall.

So, am I in despair? Obviously not, because if I am in despair or depressed, I'm still moving in the same field. So all that has stopped. Realizing that I cannot possibly do anything, make any movement, what takes place in my mind? I realize I cannot do a thing. So what has happened to the quality of my mind, which has always moved to accumulate, to become? All that has stopped. The moment I realize this – no movement. Is that possible? Or am I living in illusion? Or have I really gone through all this to come to that point? Or do I suddenly say, I must be quiet?

Is there a revolution in my mind, a revolution in the sense that movement has completely stopped? And if it has, is love something beyond the wall?

DAVID BOHM: Well, it wouldn't mean anything.

KRISHNAMURTI: Of course, it couldn't be.

DAVID BOHM: The wall itself is the product of the process which is illusion.

KRISHNAMURTI: Exactly. I'm realizing that the wall *is* this movement. So when this movement ends, that quality of intelligence, love and so on, is there. That's the whole point.

DAVID BOHM: Yes; could one say the movement ends, the movement sees that it has no point?

KRISHNAMURTI: It is like the so-called 'skill' to see a danger.

DAVID BOHM: Well, it could be.

KRISHNAMURTI: Yes. Any danger demands a certain amount of awareness. But I have never realized as a human being that the accumulating process is a tremendous danger.

DAVID BOHM: Because that seems to be the essence of security.

KRISHNAMURTI: Of course. You come along and point it out to me, and I'm listening to you very carefully and I see, and I actually perceive the danger of that. And perception is part of love, isn't it? So the very perception, without any motive, without any direction, of the wall – which has been brought into being by this movement of accumulation – *is* intelligence and love.

Brockwood Park, 16 September 1980

Index